Elena's Secrets of Mexican Cooking

ELENA ZELAYETA

Elena's
Secrets
of Mexican
Cooking

DOLPHIN BOOKS
DOUBLEDAY & COMPANY, INC., GARDEN CITY, N.Y.

To my precious granddaughter Elenita
who has been a constant joy and blessing
since she came into our lives

Dolphin Books Edition: 1973
ISBN: 0-385-00197-5
Copyright © 1958 by Prentice-Hall, Inc.
Englewood Cliffs, N.J.

Preface

I hope that the readers of this book will be as happy in using it as I have been in writing it. It is my third cookbook. I was asked to do it because of the growing interest in Mexican and Spanish food in this country. I hope that I have, in my small way, furthered that interest and that this new book will multiply it. In it I want to accomplish three things:

To those who know nothing of Mexican cuisine except what they have heard—that it's always searingly hot, exotically and overly spiced, and heavy—I hope to convince that it just *isn't* so! And to those who know something, but not everything, about South-of-the-Border food, I hope to show that tamales and enchiladas, good as they are, are not the only dishes Mexican cooks know how to prepare. And I wish to convince everyone that Mexican dishes may be served harmoniously with American ones, and that even one Mexican dish can do much to add interest to what might otherwise be a very dull meal.

First, however, I must give you a bit of the background of Mexico, as well as my own, so that you will better understand this book.

The food of Mexico reflects its history. First, there are the dishes native to the country—dishes which today are prepared very much as they were in the days of the Aztecs. These are the things that are made of *masa*—tortillas, tamales, tacos, and such (page 123)—frijoles and chiles. The ingredients of all three of these (corn, beans, and peppers) are native to Mexico and the Indians lived on them, along with game and fish and the other native plants such as chocolate, pumpkins, avocados, tomatoes, potatoes, and vanilla. Even in those early days, Mexican cooking was an art and foods were lovingly prepared with flavors skillfully blended, even as they are today.

And then came the conqueror, Cortez, with his men. Many of them sent for their families and settled in Mexico. Of course, they brought with them the favorite dishes of Spain—those made with rice, olive oil, and wine. These were good foods; so good that they were soon adopted by the Mexicans, even as the Spaniards took a liking to the native dishes. Still later, much later, Maximilian and Carlotta and their court came to Mexico. In their retinue were cooks skilled in the preparation of French, Austrian, and Italian dishes. The best of these, too, were assimilated by the Mexicans, producing a truly cosmopolitan cuisine, yet one as distinctive as any in the world.

There are five meals a day served in Mexico, though few partake of all of them. The first is *desayuno,* at which coffee or chocolate and a roll are served. Later comes a larger breakfast, really a sort of brunch. It is called *almuerzo. Comida,* the main meal of the day, is followed by the famous siesta. *Merienda* is tea-time, or perhaps I should say chocolate-time, because that is what is usually served, along with a *pan dulce,* or sweet roll, or with one of Mexico's whimsical little snacks. *Cena* is supper, and it often features soup, either liquid or dry (page 23). At this meal some dessert usually completes the meal, for Mexicans have a very sweet tooth.

In Mexico there was really no middle class, economically speaking. There was a small very wealthy class and the rest of the people were poor, at least by American standards. This, because of the adoption of modern methods in industry, will probably (and fortunately) become a thing of the past. However, this condition has had its influence on Mexican cookery, an influence that will be welcomed by American housewives on a budget. The people of Mexico have learned to make a little meat go a long way, and, by means of beautifully blended herbs and spices, to give the cheapest of foods unbelievably delicious flavor—as you will see when you try these recipes.

The dishes of Mexico, as well as the methods of preparing them and the names by which they are known, vary from state to state, from region to region. And to make it even more confusing, some Mexican dishes common in the Southwestern part of the United States, are little known in Mexico, and others, though known, bear different names. Thus you may not always find the recipe you want under the name by which you know it. However, I have tried, wherever possible, to give both names, or at least an accurate enough description so that you will recognize it.

As for me, I have been an American for many many years, but I was born in Mexico of Spanish parents. My family were innkeepers in the small town of Mineral del Oro (the gold mine), and my mother was a wonderful cook, one who knew food well and had a genius for bringing out the best in every dish. It was from her that I learned Spanish cooking. The Mexican cooks who worked at the inn taught me how to prepare *their* dishes. We came to San Francisco when I was a young girl, and because I, too, loved to cook, I soon learned how to do it in the manner of my new countrymen. I have cooked ever since—sometimes to help financially, as when I ran my restaurant in San Francisco, sometimes to cook good things for my family and friends to eat, but always for the sheer joy of being busy in the kitchen preparing old favorites and creating new ones.

Because of my many years in this country, I have learned what Americans like to eat. These recipes have been adapted to suit the palates of my American friends and my American sons, Larry and Bill. Although I have made some slight changes in my way of cooking genuine Mexican dishes—such as cutting down on the amounts of very hot chiles, and using the electric blender instead of the primitive *molcajete* still used by some Mexicans—I have made every effort to keep the recipes authentic. True, I sometimes substitute chili powder for hand-ground chiles, but then so do the Mexicans themselves. If you want your dishes hotter, simply increase the amount of chile. I have used substitutions rarely, and then only when it makes no difference in the true Mexican flavor of the food. I cannot, with honesty, substitute corn meal for *masa,* or green bell peppers for *chile poblano,* or make other changes often recommended to Americans. But, because the Mexican ingredients called for in this book are not available everywhere, I have listed some stores in various parts of the country where they can be purchased by mail (pages 4–5).

Although this book is a new one, with many hitherto unpublished recipes, I have found it necessary to repeat a few recipes from my other two books, *Elena's Famous Mexican and Spanish Recipes* and *Elena's Fiesta Recipes.* This is because no book on Mexican cuisine could possibly be without them. As for those two earlier books, I once more want to thank my friends who made them possible. In the first, I had invaluable help from a group of San Francisco home economists. I will always be grateful to them, and to my friends who have since helped to sell the little volume. The second was edited, and the charming commentaries written, by Marka Ritchie, whose husband, Ward Ritchie, published it. Thanks to them for allowing me to use some of the recipes from it.

To individually mention the many friends who helped with this book would be impossible, so I have chosen to thank them as a whole—those who retested my recipes, those who typed them, those who edited the manuscript and read it back to me, and those who did many errands necessary in the writing of a book. To them all go my deepest love and gratitude.

I hope this book will bring me new friends as have my other two. If I can be of help to any of you, if there is any question that I can answer, I will happily do so. Simply write me in care of my publisher.

ELENA ZELAYETA

San Francisco, 1958

Contents

Introduction

Elena (everybody calls her that) is the gayest, dearest bundle of energy I have ever known. She is interested in everything and everybody. Her eyes twinkle, as does her laugh. She moves quickly and surely in her kitchen, her tiny hands skillfully preparing the wonderful dishes for which she is so famous. To watch her at work, to see her quick smile as she looks at you, to hear her merry chuckle, you'd swear she had not a trouble in the world. Yet Elena is blind.

Elena's story is a fascinating one, filled as it is with love and courage, with work and with tragedy. I would like to tell it all so that you would know what a truly wonderful woman this Elena is —but this is a cookbook, so I will tell only of how Elena's love of cooking has been her salvation. Without it she would probably never have been able to keep going. Just as Elena's friends turn to her for help in their darkest moments, so Elena turns to cooking. When first she lost her eyesight, this was not easy. She was a young matron with an adoring husband and a darling baby son—her Larry—and another baby on the way. Her sight failed; it had never been really good, but now it was gone forever. Elena says now that she gave in to complete and utter despair. She says more than that—that the Elena of that time was a bitter, humorless, disagreeable woman. This I don't believe, but I do believe Elena when she says it was food that helped her out of her hopelessness. She realized that her husband and her sons, the younger one a tiny baby she had never seen, were eating food of which she was ashamed, food that was cooked by the ignorant hired girl who was all the Zelayetas could afford. Elena determined that she herself would do the cooking and care for her sons. So what did she do? She fired the girl and taught herself, by trial and many errors, how to cook in the dark. So well did she teach herself that now she sometimes demonstrates for other blind persons what she herself has learned.

First she learned to conquer fear. The kitchen was full of terror —fire, sharp knives, hot fat, can openers. She had to learn all over again how to handle them. Today, she is the one who terrifies her friends as she casually deep-fries *buñuelos,* or heats tortillas in the open flame, or bones a chicken.

She learned how to separate eggs by breaking them into the palm of her hand and letting the whites slip through her fingers; to measure liquid by pouring it over her sensitive fingers; to smell or taste any ingredient that she wasn't sure of; to always keep things in exactly the same place so that she could find them. She learned to tell the temperature of deep fat by smell, the doneness of meat by touch. She timed her cooking by 15-minute radio breaks, and gauged the heat of her oven by its feel.

She also learned to wash and iron, sew and clean. But the thing that made her happiest was that once more her family was eating her delicious food. True, she had to feel for baby Billy's mouth before she dared feed him with a spoon, and she made many mistakes when serving the meals. But by this time her wonderful sense of humor had returned and she roared with laughter when she served the salad with marmalade instead of mayonnaise because someone had switched jars on her well-arranged shelves. She even thought it hilariously funny when, entertaining some friends, she found that she had baked a spoon in her chicken pie. In short, Elena had taught herself to live again.

Then tragedy struck again. Her husband, her adored and adoring Lawrence, was killed in an automobile accident. This blow was greater than the first one, but Elena took it in a bigger stride. She had to, for now she had her sons to support. Again her cooking was her salvation. Her first book had already been written and was selling very very well. She wrote another one, an inspirational book called *Lessons in Living,* a subject that she knew only too well. She taught the blind and gave cookery lessons and inspirational talks to various clubs. But don't get me wrong—these talks I call "inspirational" for lack of a better name. They were never preachy or sanctimonious, but were always very funny. There's nothing Elena likes better than a good joke, especially if she is the butt of it. It's her very human humor that makes her so endearing.

Today, Elena's boys are grown. Larry has a little daughter named Elenita, for her grandmother. Both boys are in business with their mother in San Francisco—the food business, of course. They make, freeze, and market Elena's famous tortillas and tamales, tacos, enchiladas, and tamalitos.

Busy as she is, Elena always manages to entertain at any possible excuse. There's nothing she loves more than a party, and there is no one who knows better how to give one. She is so perfectly organized that everything runs without a hitch. She usually does all the work herself, but her delicious meals, so beautifully prepared and served, put many of us to shame. How many women do you know who can greet you at the door, poised and rested and self-assured, entertain you in the living room, and then announce that dinner is served? And, miraculously, it is.

Her job of hostess doesn't stop there. I don't know how she does it, but she seems to know exactly how much of each dish every guest has eaten. Her meals are always lavish—she has a horror of not having more than enough of everything—but don't think you can get away with eating sparingly at Elena's table. "What's the matter," she will tease, "don't you like my paella?" That's Elena for you, Elena of the loving heart, the gay laugh, the skillful fingers —brave, witty, generous Elena, who has thousands of friends and who is a best friend to every one of them.

HELEN EVANS BROWN

The ABC's of Cooking, Elena Style

Here is a brief glossary of terms you'll meet often in the recipes and an abbreviated list of stores where Mexican foods are available.

ANISE: A seed with a flavor much like licorice. Found on herb shelves in groceries. Seeds should be ground to release flavor.

CHICHARRONES: Pork cracklings highly esteemed by Mexicans as appetizers and used in many other ways as you'll discover in the recipes in this book. Found with potato chips and other nibble foods in markets.

CHILE SAUCE: Mexican stores carry a selection of red and green chile sauces. Salsa Jalapeña, Salsa de Tomatillo and Salsa de Pipián are popular.

CHILES: Peppers to you, and such a variety: green, yellow, brown, and shades of red. Run the flavor ladder from mild and sweet like the pimiento to hot and downright fiery like the Piquin, also known as the Tepin. Range in size from tiny (again like the Piquin or Tepin) to big like the Poblano. Some are used fresh or canned (Jalapeño, Pimiento, Chipotle, Poblano, Serrano, to name a few). Some are used dry (Ancho, Mulato, Pasilla, and the Piquin or Tepin, to name a few more). Peeled green chiles (the Poblano is used for these) and sweet red pimientos are usually found in 4-ounce cans or jars all over the country in groceries as well as Mexican stores.

CHILE POWDER: Very often comes under the label "chili powder," and there are many brands. Taste before you get reckless with this, because the brands vary considerably in degree of heat. The powder is compounded of dried peppers and herbs. The fresher it is, the better.

CILANTRO: Perhaps better known as "coriander." Often found fresh in Mexican or in Oriental markets where it is known as Chinese parsley. Easy to grow from seeds. When fresh is used, double the amount of dry specified. The seeds are generally available in the herb shelves of groceries. Seeds must be crushed to release flavor.

CHORIZO: Pork sausage with elevated seasoning. Available in Mexican stores (about six sausages in casings to a pound) or you can make your own, following recipe on page 89.

COMINO, CUMIN: One of the savory seeds. "Comino" is just Spanish for "cumin." You'll find it in seed or powdered form on the seasoning shelves of markets. Seeds must be ground or crushed to give the full flavor, which is really racy.

GARBANZOS: Or chick peas. Available canned in groceries. Dried variety harder to find, but most Mexican stores have them.

JACK CHEESE: Creamy, white rich cheese popular in California. A poor traveler, so not found too many places out of the state. Wisconsin brick or a mild Cheddar may be substituted.

LONGANIZA: Spanish sausage, well-liked by Mexicans. Milder than chorizo and like Italian linguica. Found in Mexican stores and some fancy food markets.

MANGO: Exotic fruit tasting rather like a pineapple-peach combine. Common in Mexico as apples here and used similarly in jam, jellies, butters, salads, desserts. Now found in green groceries fresh, as well as canned, in many food stores. Canned mangoes are more common, but the fresh ones (good eaten out-of-hand, peeled and eaten as a banana) are moving into markets across the land. (More in dessert chapter.)

MASA: Moist, fresh-ground Mexican corn preparation. Can be purchased fresh at Mexican stores. American-made masa flour is available in many groceries. Ask your grocer to order it, if he doesn't stock it. Lots more about this in the chapter devoted to it.

MOLE: This is the sauce used for the great festival dish, Turkey in Mole Sauce (page 61). Commercially prepared in powder or liquid form in Mexican groceries as Mole Poblano, Mole Verde, Pipian Ranchero.

MONTEREY JACK CHEESE: See Jack Cheese.

NOPALES: Leaves of the prickly pear cactus. Available canned in Mexican groceries. Sometimes labelled "Nopalitos."

ORÉGANO: Spanish name for wild marjoram and a favorite herb in Spain and Mexico. In dry form, should be rubbed between palms of hands to get full flavor benefit. Fresh orégano (it's easy to grow) leaves should be minced. Double the amount of dried orégano called for when fresh is used.

PAPAYA: Tropical fruit now in markets throughout U. S. Used for salads, desserts, appetizers, fresh and canned. Eaten like melon, which it resembles in taste. Ready to eat fresh when half yellow and yields to gentle hand pressure.

PINE NUTS: Small, soft nuts of several varieties of evergreens. Available at nut stores and groceries.

TOMATILLO: A tomato-like vegetable. Sometimes available fresh in Mexican stores, usually available canned. Distinctive flavor is very important in some Mexican dishes.

TORTILLA: Thin corn cake. The bread of Mexico. Ready-made now and available in Mexican stores as well as many groceries. Also found canned.

TOMATO SAUCE: Available in grocery stores everywhere, usually in 8-ounce cans.

SALSA JALAPEÑA: See Chile Sauce.

SALSA DE TOMATILLO: See Chile Sauce.

Here's where these Mexican foods may be purchased. No attempt was made to have a complete list of all stores handling Mexican food products. There are ever so many more, especially in Texas, New Mexico, and Arizona. Here are some which you might write to if you can't find the magic ingredients for these recipes in your town:

LOS ANGELES: La Luz del Dia, 610 North Spring Street
NEW YORK: Casa Moneo, 219 West 14th Street
SAN FRANCISCO: Mi Rancho Market, 3365 20th Avenue
WASHINGTON, D. C.: La Sevillana, 2469 18th Street N. W.
                  Pena, 1636 17th Street N. W.

YUMA: Joe Chrepin, 485 15th Street
BOSTON: S. S. Pierce Company, 133 Brookline Avenue
PASADENA: La Luz del Dia, 720 South Fair Oak
CHICAGO: El Fenix, 813 South Halsted
             Casa Esteiro Importers, 1103 South Halsted
             El Milagro Grocers, 1114 South Halsted

Aperitivos

❦ (Appetizers)

Mexico has many flavorsome little tidbits that are just right to serve as appetizers. My most popular ones are tamalitos (miniature tamales), empanadas, carnitas, and tostaditas, but I am glad to say that I have never known any of them to go begging. That's probably because they are a change from the usual American variety. In the beverage section (pages 233–241) you will find some of the drinks that Mexicans serve with them.

COCTÉL DE ABULÓN

(Abalone Cocktail)

I use canned abalone for this appetizer. It tastes quite different from the fresh shellfish, but it is very good eating and is available in fancy markets all over the country. Fresh abalone can be had only in Mexico and California.

Dice the meat of canned abalone, add its own juices and season with lemon or lime juice to taste. Chill well and serve with salsa Jalapeña on the side so that guests can add their own. This sauce is as hot as el diablo. Serves 6.

BOCADITOS DE ABULÓN

(Abalone Tidbits)

Fix the abalone as above but have the cubes a little larger and impale each on a toothpick. Have the sauce, seasoned with the Jalapeña, nearby for dunking. Makes about 12 servings.

GUACAMOLE

(Avocado Dip)

Guacamole, well known in the United States, is a versatile dish. It is wonderful as a cocktail dip with tortilla chips (tostaditas) or crackers, but it is also wonderful on lettuce, as an accompaniment for meat or fish, and for such Mexican snacks as tacos and tostadas. And do try filling miniature cream puffs or tart shells with it.

2 *very ripe medium-sized avocados*

2 *medium-sized tomatoes*

1 *medium-sized onion, or 1 bunch green onions, chopped*

Salsa Jalapeña or green peeled chiles, chopped

Wine vinegar or lemon juice to taste

Salt to taste

Mash avocados with a fork, not too smooth, and add the other ingredients. If you can't serve it at once, cover closely with Saran wrap or foil, as it darkens when exposed to the air, but do not try to make it too far ahead of time. Add the salsa Jalapeña or chiles to taste, and make sure you use plenty of salt. Vary this dish by adding pomegranate seeds, or fresh cilantro (coriander, or Chinese parsley), chopped peanuts, or bits of crisp bacon, or chicharrones. Makes 3 cups of spread.

SALSA DE AGUAGATE PARA SOPEAR

(Avocado Dip)

1 (8 oz.) package cream
    cheese
2 tablespoons finely-chopped
    onion
1 large avocado

1 tablespoon fresh lime or
    lemon juice
¾ teaspoon seasoned salt
    Dash Tabasco sauce

Soften cream cheese and add onion. Cut avocado into halves and remove seed and skin. Force fruit through a sieve, or blend in electric blender. Mix with all remaining ingredients. Use as a dip for chips or crackers. Makes about 1 pint.

SALSA DE POLLO Y AGUACATE PARA SOPEAR

(Chicken and Avocado Dip)

2 avocados, mashed
1 cooked chicken breast, very
    finely chopped
2 teaspoons lemon juice

Salsa Jalapeña, as much as
    desired
Salt to taste

Combine all ingredients well but do not beat. Use this as a dip or spread it on rounds of toast. It is also good on miniature fried tortillas or tostaditas, topped with shredded lettuce, sprinkled with French dressing and garnished with sliced stuffed olives. Makes about 2 cups.

CARNITAS

(Little Meats)

No one could love Carnitas more than my dear doctor, Milton Greengard. Last time I served them to him—and believe me, I have to include them in my menu when he comes for dinner—I tripled the recipe. He still wanted more!

2 pounds lean pork   *Salt and pepper to taste*
½ teaspoon MSG

Cut the pork into 1-inch cubes, sprinkle with MSG, salt and pepper and let stand for an hour or so. Place in a shallow baking pan in a 300°F. oven for about 2 hours, pouring off the fat as it accumulates. Serve hot with tostadas and guacamole, or as is, impaled on wooden picks. These freeze beautifully. Serves eight.

* MSG is Monosodium Glutamate, marketed under trade-names Accent and Enhance.

BISCUITS DE FIESTA

(Fiesta Biscuits)

These may not sound Mexican, but I assure you they are. You'd be surprised at the number of South-of-the-Border cooks who use our American mixes, but they always add their own special touches. These freeze nicely.

For appetizers split tiny biscuits while hot and spread with cheese or deviled ham. Or, make a depression in the center of each biscuit and fill with Chile Butter, made by blending ¼ cup soft butter and ½ teaspoon chile powder.

2 tablespoons butter
2 cups biscuit mix
⅔ cup milk
2 tablespoons finely-chopped
   onion

2 tablespoons finely-chopped
   green pepper
2 tablespoons finely-chopped
   pimiento

Cut butter into biscuit mix. Add all remaining ingredients and mix to moderately stiff dough. Roll out on lightly-floured board and cut with tiny biscuit cutter for appetizer biscuits (about 1-inch diameter) or use 2-inch cutter for larger biscuits. Bake in a 450°F. oven until lightly browned, about 8 to 10 minutes. Serve as appetizers or to accompany soup or salad. Makes 3 dozen tiny or 1½ dozen larger biscuits.

ALBONDIGUITAS

(Little Meat Balls)

Could be I'm prejudiced, but I think these tiny meat balls have it all over the better known Swedish variety. Try them and see if you agree.

1 pound finely-ground lean
   beef
1 cup fine bread crumbs
1 egg, beaten
¾ cup half and half (milk and
   cream)
1 small onion, minced

1 tablespoon butter or
   margarine
1 or more tablespoons chile
   chipotle, chopped
½ teaspoon orégano
Salt
Butter and oil for frying

Combine all ingredients and mix thoroughly. Shape into balls the size of a cherry. Fry in heavy skillet in mixture of butter and oil. When browned, put into chafing dish to keep warm. Serve with toothpicks. This yields from 60 to 70 meat balls. These freeze wonderfully.

CAZUELITAS

(Little Casseroles)

For something very different, try these on your cocktail guests. Since this is almost impossible to translate, I've used an English term based on their shape—that of a small casserole.

1 pound fresh masa (or masa ½ *teaspoon salt*
 flour) * ⅓ *cup grated Parmesan cheese*

Combine all ingredients and mix thoroughly. Divide into 24 balls. Press thumb into center of each ball and with the fingers shape into a little deep dish (cazuelita). Fry in deep fat or oil until golden brown. These cazuelitas may be filled with refried beans, sprinkled with grated cheese, then a layer of meat, chicken or fish, with shredded and finely chopped lettuce on top of all. Garnish with little pieces of green chile or chile chipotle. They freeze nicely before being filled.

* See page 123.

PASTELITOS PARA COCTÉL

(Pastry for Cocktails)

Your friends will probably think these are filled with something bland like chicken salad. Imagine their surprise when they bite into this delectable tidbit. These are actually little cream puff shells, but I do not know the name in Spanish.

Puffs:

¾ *cup water*   ¾ *cup sifted all-purpose flour*
 6 *tablespoons butter or* 3 *eggs*
  margarine   *Grated Parmesan cheese*

Heat water and butter to boiling. Add flour all at once and cook, stirring, until mixture forms a ball that follows spoon around the pan. Remove from heat, and add eggs, one at a time, beating thoroughly after each addition. Drop by small teaspoonfuls onto ungreased baking sheet, and sprinkle with grated Parmesan cheese. Bake in 400°F. oven about 30 minutes, until puffed and dry. Cool. Just before serving, split one side and put a heaping teaspoonful of filling in each puff. These shells, before filling, freeze nicely. Makes about 3 dozen tiny puffs.

Filling:

1 (8 oz.) package cream
    cheese
1 teaspoon chicken stock base
    or 1 chicken bouillon cube,
    crumbled

1 tablespoon finely chopped
    onion
¼ cup cream
½ cup ripe olive pieces
1 tablespoon chopped green
    chiles

Soften cheese. Mix in chicken stock base, onion and cream. Stir in olives and green chiles.

CANAPÉS DE JAMÓN

(Ham Canapés)

I first had these served to me in Mexico City and foolishly, I didn't beg, borrow, or steal the recipe. However, I think I've worked it out with the expert help of my ever faithful friend, Dorothy Canet.

Pastry:

1½ cups sifted all-purpose
    flour
1 teaspoon salt
1½ teaspoons celery seed

½ cup shortening
⅓ cup cold water
2 tablespoons soft butter or
    margarine

Sift flour and salt into bowl and add celery seed. Cut in shortening and add just enough water to make dough hold together. Roll out on floured board into an oblong, about ¼-inch thick. Spread with butter. Fold in half, then in thirds, making six layers. Chill thoroughly. Roll out dough until about ¼-inch thick. Bake in 450°F. oven until golden brown, about 12 to 15 minutes. Cool. Cover with topping. Serve hot, cut in small squares, sticks or diamonds. Makes 3 dozen appetizers. These freeze beautifully.

Topping:

4 thin slices boiled ham
¼ cup chopped green peeled chiles
½ cup tomato catsup
1 cup sliced Monterey Jack or Cheddar cheese

Cut ham in small squares and arrange over baked pastry. Mix green chiles and catsup and spoon over ham. Cover with cheese and place under broiler until melted.

MANTEQUILLA DE CAMARÓN

(Shrimp Butter)

Keep a jar of this in your refrigerator. It is as good for a sandwich filling as it is for an appetizer spread.

1 (5 oz.) can shrimp, or 1 cup cooked fresh shrimp
¼ cup soft butter or margarine
½ teaspoon prepared mustard
½ teaspoon Worcestershire sauce
Dash Tabasco sauce
¼ cup finely chopped onion
1½ tablespoons lemon juice

Clean shrimp and chop finely. Cream butter and blend in mustard, Worcestershire sauce, Tabasco sauce, onion and lemon juice.

Blend in chopped shrimp. Use as a spread for tostaditas or crackers. Makes 1 cup of spread.

FRIJOLES PARA SOPEAR

(Bean Dip)

Bean dip, put up in cans, has become very popular of late. Here is a much less expensive, and I think, much tastier version.

Thoroughly mash 1 cup refried beans (page 114) and combine with 1 cup sour cream. Mix well and add as much salsa Jalapeña as desired. This makes a delightful dip for tostaditas.

TOMATITOS CON OSTIONES

(Plum Tomatoes with Oysters)

These are called plum tomatoes or cherry tomatoes depending on where you live.

Cut a plum tomato in half with a sharp knife and insert a smoked oyster. Secure oyster by sticking a toothpick through tomato.

CHILE CON QUESO PARA SOPEAR

(Green Chile with Cheese Dip)

Americans all fall in love with Chile con Queso. In spite of the chile it isn't searingly hot, but just pleasantly flavorsome. I am crazy about it.

Chile con Queso is a good dunk. Follow recipe on page 186. Keep warm over chafing dish and serve with tostaditas.

BOCADILLOS DE OSTIONES A LA MEXICANA

(Oyster Morsels, Mexican Style)

These certainly are a "good mouthful." You can make them with crab, shrimp, or lobster in place of the oysters. Any way, they are superb.

Recipe for Empanadas #1, page 173.

1 tablespoon oil
1 small onion, minced
1 medium-sized tomato, peeled and chopped

1 (7 oz.) can oysters, coarsely chopped
1 tablespoon capers
1 tablespoon chopped parsley
Salt and pepper

Wilt onion in hot oil, add tomato, cook a few minutes. Add oysters, capers, parsley, salt and pepper. Mix well. Cool.

Roll out empanada dough ⅛-inch thick; cut out rounds 1½ inches in diameter; place filling in center of a round; wet edges and cover with another round of dough. Seal firmly and fry in deep hot oil until brown, or bake at 400°F. for 10 to 12 minutes. Makes about 12 bocadillos. These will freeze.

CAMARÓN ENDIABLADO

(Deviled Shrimp)

Here is an appetizer with authority.

½ cup white table wine
½ cup wine vinegar
1 teaspoon prepared
    horseradish
2 tablespoons prepared
    mustard
2 tablespoons tomato catsup

1 tablespoon paprika
¼ teaspoon cayenne pepper
1 teaspoon salt
1 crushed clove garlic
1 cup salad oil
1 pound cleaned, cooked
    shrimp

Combine first 9 ingredients with salad oil and beat until well blended. Pour over shrimp and marinate at least several hours in refrigerator. When ready to serve, drain shrimp and arrange on lettuce-lined bowl. Makes 6 to 8 servings.

ALBONDIGUITAS DE POLLO Y JAMÓN

(Chicken and Ham Balls)

Wilma Sledge—I call her my adopted daughter because I love her as if she really were mine—gave me this recipe.

1 breast of chicken, cooked
¼ pound ham
1 slice bread
2 eggs

1 or more tablespoons chopped
    chile chipotle
Fine bread crumbs
Oil for frying

Grind together chicken, ham, bread and chile chipotle. Add eggs and mix well. Shape into small balls, roll in bread crumbs and fry in small amount of oil until browned on all sides. Serve hot as appetizers. These may be cooked ahead, kept in freezer and re-heated in the oven when ready to serve. Will freeze beautifully before or after cooking. Makes 60 to 70 small balls.

TIRITAS DE COCO

(Toasted Coconut Strips)

The Mexicans no doubt borrowed this idea from the Islands, but now it's theirs to keep.

Poke holes in the three soft areas at top of coconut shell with an ice pick or other sharp instrument; drain milk. Crack shell open. Run small sharp knife between hard outer shell and inner meat. Pry meat from shell. It isn't necessary to remove the thin brown skin unless you wish to. Cut coconut meat into thin strips using a vegetable parer or sharp knife. Arrange in single layer on shallow pan or cooky sheet. Sprinkle lightly with salt, if desired. Toast in a 300°F. oven until golden brown, watching to prevent too deep browning. Stir gently once or twice so strips will toast as evenly as possible. Cool and store in an airtight container. One small coconut makes about 1 quart toasted strips.

Serve as a cocktail appetizer or between-meal nibbler. You may also crush the toasted strips and serve sprinkled over ice cream or on frosted cakes or wherever toasted coconut could be used. Tastes good with creamed chicken or on chicken salads, and makes a fine accompaniment for curried dishes.

CANAPÉS DE CHORIZO Y QUESO

(Chorizo and Cheese Canapés)

These are so good that I serve them as an appetizer or as an ac-companiment to soups or salads. Watch the men go for them.

½ *pound chorizo*
4 *green onions, chopped*
1 *can tomato paste*
½ *teaspoon orégano*
1 *tablespoon chopped chile*
   chipotle (*more if*
   desired)

Grated Parmesan cheese
½ *pound Monterey Jack or*
   Cheddar cheese, thinly
   sliced
Salt

Remove chorizo from case; fry without added fat until browned. Add onion and cook a few minutes longer. Add tomato paste, orégano, chile, and salt to taste; cook a few minutes longer. Spread on split French rolls or on slices of French bread. Sprinkle generously with Parmesan cheese, then cover with sliced cheese. Cut to desired size and place under broiler or bake in hot oven until cheese is melted and bubbly. This amount is sufficient for 3 rolls. They keep well.

ROLLITOS DE JAIBA

(Crab Rolls)

This recipe came from the home economics department at Pacific Gas & Electric, via my wonderful friend of many years, Marguerite Fenner, who heads the department.

1 (6½ oz.) *can crab meat*
1 *egg, beaten*
½ *cup tomato juice*
1 *cup bread crumbs*
½ *teaspoon salt*

1 *teaspoon chile powder*
2 *teaspoons prepared*
   mustard
1 *teaspoon chopped parsley*

Flake crab meat and remove any bones. Add egg, tomato juice, crumbs, and seasonings; chill in refrigerator 2 to 3 hours. Form mixture into finger-sized pieces. Arrange on broiler rack over pan and broil 6 inches from source of heat, 5 minutes to each side. Serve with toothpicks. Makes about two dozen.

ACEITUNAS RELLENAS A LA ELENA

(My Stuffed Olives)

These take patience but they are worth it.

1 (7½ oz.) can pitted olives	⅓ cup wine vinegar
1 (¾ oz.) can anchovy fillets, cut in small pieces	1 tablespoon olive oil Oil from anchovies
1 can pimientos, chopped	¼ cup minced parsley
1 clove garlic, mashed or pressed	

Drain olives and stuff with the anchovy fillets. Combine the other ingredients, except parsley; pour over the olives and marinate overnight. Mix in parsley half an hour before serving. If the idea of stuffing the olives throws you, don't do it. Simply add the anchovies to the marinade and pour over the olives. These will keep for a week or more if parsley is added just before serving.

PICO DE GALLO

(Rooster's Bill)

The jicama is a bland fruit that is not always available in this country, but the combination of the orange and chile, in itself, is so truly appetizing that I couldn't resist including it. I can't think of a better way to begin a meal, especially a Mexican one. Remember, though, that chile piquin is hotter than the well known hinges, so take it easy when you add it!

3 cups chopped jicama   Powdered chile piquin
2 cups chopped orange   Salt
  Juice of 2 lemons

Mix all ingredients, except chile, together. Chill thoroughly and
serve in cocktail glasses with a judicious sprinkling of chile piquin
on top.

SALSA DE REQUESÓN PARA SOPEAR

(Cottage Cheese Sauce for Dipping)

My pet name for this is "Lou's Firecracker Dip," because one
of my pet friends, Lou Richardson, originated this zippy sauce and
so dubbed it. It is a moderately thin dip, and it makes a fine dressing
for wedges of lettuce.

1 pint creamed cottage cheese   ½ teaspoon salt
1 can green peeled chiles   1 teaspoon seasoned salt
1 tablespoon salsa Jalapeña   2 teaspoons lemon juice
  (or your favorite green
  chile relish)

Mix all ingredients in blender until smooth. Makes about 2 cups.
Serve with tortilla chips or potato chips or crackers.

TORTITAS COMPUESTAS

(Fancy Buns)

In Mexico these are sold in open-air stands and are very popular
as snacks. The homemade kind are great favorites at picnics. In
Mexico they use the rolls that are called "bolillos" because they are

pointed at the ends like a shuttle used for making lace. Probably the nearest things we have north of the border are crusty French or Italian rolls. However, when serving these as an appetizer, I use tiny round rolls that I make myself or order from a bakery.

Split rolls in half and spread the cut sides with well-mashed refried beans. Sprinkle with grated Romano or Parmesan cheese, then top with chopped cooked chicken or sardines, tuna or canned salmon that has been mashed and seasoned with lemon juice, minced onion and salsa Jalapeña. Now add finely-shredded lettuce and guacamole. Garnish with a slice of pimiento-stuffed olive. If you are taking these on a picnic, use larger rolls and carry the lettuce, guacamole, and olives separately, to be added on the spot.

Sopas

🎵 (Soups)

If you think that all soups are liquid or *aguada* as the Spanish say, you don't know Sopas Secas, the dry soups of Mexico, which are made with rice, pastes, or even tortillas. They are cooked in stock, like any soup, but cooked until all the rich broth has been absorbed. In Mexico they are served right after the ordinary, or liquid soup, but only on festive occasions.

My boys are very fond of soups. Like their father, they do not feel a meal is complete without it. I always keep several quarts of stock in my freezer, ready for any emergency. And I assure you that it's good rich stock, chock full of flavor. I remember my mother's favorite proverb she used to quote when making soup.

"Bien cocina la moza pero mejor la bolsa" which means "The kitchen maid cooks well, but the pocketbook cooks better." How true. When making good soups you cannot be skimpy!

MANERA DE HACER UN BUEN CALDO

(Manner of making a rich broth)

Chicken: Select a large stewing hen; have it disjointed and cleaned. For each 1½ pounds of chicken use 1 quart cold water. Bring water and chicken slowly to boiling point and skim. Add salt, 1 onion, 2 cloves of garlic, 3 or 4 stalks of celery, and 2 or 3 leeks. Cover and simmer until chicken is tender—about 2 hours or more, depending on weight of the chicken. Cool and refrigerate; skim fat from the top and strain broth. (I use the chicken in any number of ways.)

Beef: The same amount and proportions as for chicken broth (1½ pounds of chuck, brisket, or rump to each quart of cold water), only I add marrow bones and I use 1 onion, 2 cloves of garlic, ¼ teaspoon of whole pepper, a small bay leaf, and salt to taste. If you desire a brown broth, sear the meat in a small amount of oil.

Spanish people make their broth in the same manner, but they always add a ham hock.

SOPA DE ESPUMA

(Foam Soup)

When I had my restaurant, "Elena's Mexican Village," this was a soup that my patrons always asked for. This may seem like a lot of broth, but the "light as foam" dumplings absorb a large amount of liquid.

¼ cup butter (½ bar)	2 tablespoons grated cheese
¾ cup sifted all-purpose flour	4 quarts well-seasoned
1 teaspoon baking powder	chicken broth
3 large eggs	½ cup tomato sauce

Melt the butter; add the sifted flour and baking powder. Mix well, then add the eggs, one at a time, beating well after each addition. Blend in the grated cheese. Heat broth and tomato sauce to boiling, and drop the mixture into it by teaspoonfuls. Cover the pan tightly and cook for 10 minutes without raising the cover. Will freeze beautifully. Serves 6 to 8.

COCIDO

(Mexican Boiled Dinner)

This Mexican soup is a meal in itself. Serve it with hot tortillas, or crusty rolls, and some fruit and cheese for dessert, and ask your most discriminating friends to join you for a glorious repast. The corn is eaten in the fingers.

2 pounds beef shanks	3 carrots, sliced
3 quarts water	3 zucchini, sliced
2 cloves garlic	½ pound green beans, cut up
1 onion, sliced	3 ears of corn (fresh or
8 peppercorns	frozen) cut into 1-inch
Salt to taste	pieces

Start the meat in cold water. Make a rich broth by cooking it slowly with garlic, onion, pepper, and salt. When the meat is tender, strain off the broth into another kettle, add the vegetables, corn last, and cook slowly until tender. Add the meat, cut in cubes, to the soup. If extra piquancy is desired, you may serve this with Jalapeña sauce.

SOPA DE TORTILLA

(Tortilla Soup)

It's worth rounding up some fresh cilantro (coriander) for this soup. If you haven't a Mexican store nearby, go to a Chinese one and ask for Chinese parsley (or *yinsoi-ts'oi*), or plant some seeds from your spice cabinet and wait a month for your soup.

6 tortillas
¼ cup oil
1 onion, chopped
¼ cup tomato purée
2 quarts broth, chicken or
    beef

1 teaspoon fresh cilantro
    (coriander)
Sprig of mint leaves
Grated cheese

Cut tortillas into strips about the size of macaroni, fry in oil until crisp, then remove from pan and drain on absorbent paper. Place in pot and add boiling broth which has been prepared in the following manner: Fry onion and tomato purée in the oil which was used in frying the tortillas. Add stock. Mash the cilantro, add a little broth, and strain into the stock. Cook half an hour, adding the mint leaves during the last 10 minutes. Serve with grated cheese. Serves 6.

SOPA DE ALBÓNDIGAS DE PESCADO

(Fish Ball Soup)

I first used this recipe in my book, *Elena's Famous Mexican and Spanish Recipes*. As so many readers liked it, I repeat it here.

1 large halibut head and trimmings	8 whole black peppercorns
3 quarts water	1 bay leaf
1 large onion	Salt and pepper
2 cloves garlic	¼ cup tomato purée
1 tablespoon orégano	2 large potatoes, cubed

Simmer the first 8 ingredients together about 30 minutes, until a rich broth has been made. Strain. Cook the tomato purée and potatoes in oil for 5 minutes and add the strained broth. Let simmer while you make the fish balls as follows:

1½ pounds halibut	1 teaspoon orégano
2 eggs, beaten	Salt and pepper

Remove bones and grind raw halibut; add remaining ingredients and mix well. Roll into balls about the size of a walnut. Drop into boiling broth and cook, tightly covered, 30 minutes. Serves 6 to 8.

MINGUICHE

(Sour Cream Soup)

This recipe is in my book, *Elena's Fiesta Recipes,* but it's so good that I must repeat it. It is from the state of Jalisco, and is served there during Lent. I like it any time of the year.

1 tablespoon butter
1 medium-sized onion, cut in rings
1 long green chile or ½ bell pepper, diced

1 quart sour cream
¼ cup milk
Salt and pepper to taste
¼ pound Monterey Jack cheese, cubed

Melt butter and cook onion rings and chile or pepper until tender, about 10 minutes. Add sour cream and milk, season, and heat thoroughly. A few minutes before serving, add the cheese. Serves 5 or 6.

SOPA DE ALMEJAS A LA ESPAÑOLA

(Spanish-Style Clam Soup)

2½ dozen clams
1 large onion, minced
2 cloves of garlic, minced
4 tablespoons olive oil

¼ cup minced parsley
½ cup tomato sauce
Salt and pepper

Wash clams thoroughly; add 1 cup of boiling salted water, cover and cook until shells open. Remove from shells and, if large, chop coarsely. Strain juice through double cheesecloth to remove sand. (If you want to eliminate all this work, simply use canned clams and juice.) Wilt onion in oil, add garlic, parsley, and tomato sauce. Now add clams and broth, season with salt and pepper to taste and heat thoroughly. This will freeze. Serves 4.

SOPA DE TOMATE Y AGUACATE

(Fresh Tomato and Avocado Soup)

This cold soup is wonderful for a hot day when appetites aren't keen. It's deliciously tempting, yet hearty.

6 medium-sized firm tomatoes, 1 bay leaf
  chopped   1 clove garlic
6 green onions, chopped   3 cups beef broth
6 peppercorns   1 diced avocado
1 teaspoon salt   Lemon wedges
1 teaspoon sugar   ½ cup sour cream

Combine tomato, onions, and seasonings. Sieve tomato mixture and add to broth. Chill thoroughly. Spoon into bowls and add avocado. Serve with lemon wedges and sour cream sprinkled with salt. Makes 4 to 5 servings.

SOPA DE LENTEJAS

(Lentil Soup)

If you can't get *longaniza* sausage, use the Italian *linguica*. Or, if you can't get either, use good old American hot dogs.

1 cup lentils   ½ bay leaf
1 quart water $\frac{1}{16}$ teaspoon powdered thyme
2 teaspoons salt   1 cup canned tomatoes
½ cup finely-chopped onion 2 tablespoons butter or
1 carrot, diced   margarine
1 stalk celery, diced   ¼ pound longaniza, sliced

Rinse lentils, add water, salt, onion, carrot, celery, bay leaf, and thyme. Heat to boiling, cover and cook slowly about 45 minutes. Add tomatoes, butter, and sliced longaniza, and heat. Will freeze. Serves 6 to 8.

SOPA DE ARROZ CON GALLINA

(Rice Chicken Soup)

This is one of my very favorite soups. I love to serve it at a soup party with tortillas, filled with guacamole, and Flan (page 207) for dessert.

4 tablespoons oil	*2 quarts seasoned chicken*
1 cup uncooked rice	*broth, hot*
1 medium onion, minced	*Pieces of cooked chicken*
½ cup tomato sauce	

Heat oil and brown rice lightly in it; add onion, tomato sauce and broth. Cover tightly and simmer for 30 minutes. During the last 10 minutes of cooking, add chicken—amount depending on your taste or how much you have on hand. Will freeze. Serves 6 to 8.

SOPA ESPAÑOLA DE GARBANZOS

(Spanish Garbanzo Soup)

Garbanzos, or chick peas, are great favorites with the Mexicans. This is one of those soups that men like, filled as it is with flavor and good things. If you can't find *longaniza,* use *linguica.*

½ pound dried garbanzo	*1 teaspoon paprika*
beans	*1 medium-sized onion,*
1 tablespoon salt	*minced*
1 beef bone	*1 pound potatoes, peeled and*
1 ham bone	*quartered*
2½ quarts water	*½ pound longaniza, sliced*
¼ pound salt pork, cut in	*Salt*
pieces	

Soak garbanzos overnight in water to cover and 1 tablespoon salt. Drain, add fresh water, ham and beef bones and salt. Cover and simmer for about 1 hour, or until garbanzos are almost tender. Fry the salt pork, onion, and paprika; cook a few minutes and add to the garbanzos; cover again and simmer for half an hour longer. Add potatoes, cook until they are tender, then add longaniza. Cook a few minutes longer and serve. This will freeze. Serves 6 to 8.

SOPA CREMA DE CALABACITAS

(Cream of Zucchini Soup)

So you don't like zucchini? All right, use any other vegetable or combination of vegetables. Spinach, perhaps, or peas, or carrots *and* peas. Get the idea?

1 pound zucchini	*3 cups milk*
Water to cover	*1 cup rich cream*
½ teaspoon sugar	*Salt and pepper*
1 tablespoon butter	*Chopped pimiento*
1 tablespoon flour	

Cook zucchini in water with sugar and salt until tender. Now purée it, using the water in which it was cooked. Melt butter; add flour, stirring to blend. When it starts to brown, add milk, the puréed zucchini, salt and pepper. Add cream a few minutes before serving and garnish with chopped pimiento. Serves 4.

SOPA DE FIDEO AGUADA

(Liquid Vermicelli Soup)

Fideo, as it is called in Mexico, is popular there. If you like a finer paste, use cappellini. This soup could also be made with strips of fried tortillas in place of the paste, and a sprinkle of chopped mint leaves would give it a delightful flavor.

½ pound vermicelli
Oil for frying
1 medium-sized onion, chopped
2 fresh tomatoes, peeled and chopped, or 1 cup solid-pack tomatoes, chopped

2 tablespoons chopped parsley
2 quarts chicken or beef broth, seasoned

Fry vermicelli in hot oil in kettle until golden brown, separating with a fork while frying to make sure it browns evenly. Remove vermicelli from oil and drain on absorbent paper. Remove all but 1 tablespoon oil and wilt onion in it; add tomatoes; cook a few minutes; then put in parsley and broth. When it comes to a boil, add vermicelli, cover and cook until tender. Delightful served sprinkled with grated cheese and hot tortillas on the side. Serves 6 to 8.

SOPA CON BOLITAS DE POLLO Y JAMÓN

(Soup with Chicken and Ham Balls)

Don't get the idea that these are ordinary chicken and ham balls. They are really extra special!

1 breast of chicken, cooked
¼ pound ham
1 slice bread

2 eggs
2 quarts your favorite chicken broth, seasoned

Grind chicken, ham, and bread together. Combine with eggs and mix well. Shape into small balls and drop into hot broth. Simmer for 15 to 20 minutes. Makes 28 to 30 balls.

ARROZ CON CAMARÓN

(Rice with Shrimps)

This is a *sopa seca*—it can be varied by adding peas and/or ham or bits of crisply cooked pork, or chorizo. It would make a good casserole.

½ cup oil
1 clove garlic
1 cup uncooked rice
2 tablespoons minced onion
½ cup tomato sauce

1 (4 oz.) can wet-pack shrimp
2½ cups boiling water, including liquid from shrimps
Salt and pepper

Fry garlic in oil a few minutes. Discard garlic and in the same oil, fry the rice until golden brown. Pour off excess oil, add onion, tomato sauce, shrimps, liquid, salt and pepper. Cover and simmer for 30 minutes, or until all liquid has been absorbed. Serves 6.

SOPA DE ALBÓNDIGAS

(Meat Ball Soup)

You don't have to be Mexican to enjoy this soup. It's a lusty-gusty one, and may be even more so if peas and sliced carrots are added to it along with the *albóndigas,* or meat balls.

Broth

1 onion, minced
1 clove garlic, minced
2 tablespoons oil
½ can tomato sauce
3 quarts beef stock

Albóndigas

¾ pound ground beef
¾ pound ground pork
⅓ cup raw rice
1½ teaspoons salt
¼ teaspoon pepper
1 egg, slightly beaten
1 tablespoon chopped mint leaves

Wilt onion and garlic in oil; add tomato sauce and beef stock. Heat to boiling point. Mix meat with rice, egg, mint, salt and pepper, and shape into little balls. Drop into boiling broth. Cover tightly and cook 30 minutes. Will freeze nicely. Serves 6 to 8.

SOPA SECA CON HONGOS

(Dry Soup with Mushrooms)

This is another *sopa seca,* and a mighty good one, too. Americans like to serve it as a casserole.

½ cup salad oil
½ pound vermicelli
1 tablespoon minced onion
¾ cup canned tomatoes
1 (4 oz.) can mushroom
    stems and pieces or ½

pound fresh sautéed
    mushrooms
2 cups chicken broth
½ teaspoon MSG*
Salt to taste
1 cup coarsely shredded
    Cheddar cheese

Heat the oil in a large, heavy skillet. Add uncooked vermicelli and sauté until golden brown, stirring gently with a fork while cooking to prevent its becoming too dark. Remove the vermicelli to a 2-quart casserole, pouring off all but 2 tablespoons of oil from the skillet. Add the minced onion to this oil and cook until golden, then add the tomatoes, mushrooms (including liquid), chicken broth, and seasonings. Heat all to boiling and pour over vermicelli. Cover tightly and bake in a 300°F. oven for 45 minutes. Sprinkle cheese over the top and continue baking, uncovered, 15 minutes longer. Serves 8.

* MSG is Monosodium Glutamate, marketed under trade-names Accent and Enhance.

SOPA DE PURÉ DE PAPAS

(Purée of Potato Soup)

Papas in Mexico are not what you may think. They're potatoes, and this recipe is a favorite way of using them. Call this cream of potato soup, if you'd rather.

4 medium-sized potatoes, peeled and quartered	¼ teaspoon dry mustard
1 medium-sized onion, finely chopped	1 teaspoon Worcestershire sauce
2 cups water	1 tablespoon finely chopped parsley
2½ teaspoons salt	2½ to 3 cups rich milk
¼ cup diced lean bacon (about 2 slices)	½ cup grated Parmesan or Romano cheese
½ teaspoon nutmeg	

To potatoes add onion, water, and cook until the potatoes are done. Drain, reserving water. Mash and sieve the potatoes until smooth. Fry the bacon until brown and add, along with the drippings, to the potatoes. Add milk to the potato water to make 3 cups and combine all ingredients except cheese. Heat, stirring, until piping hot. Serve with sprinkling of cheese over each serving. Makes about 2 quarts.

SOPA SECA DE TORTILLA

(Dry Tortilla Soup)

This *sopa seca* makes a good casserole to serve with charcoal broiled meats.

6 tortillas	1 bay leaf
½ cup oil	1 teaspoon orégano
1 onion, minced	Salt and pepper to taste
2 cups tomato purée	Grated cheese
6 hard-cooked eggs, sliced	

Cut tortillas into strips like macaroni. Fry in oil until crisp. Set aside to drain on brown paper. Fry minced onion in oil in which tortillas were fried. Add tomato purée. Season and cook, covered, 30 minutes. Butter a casserole. Place in layers: tortilla strips, sauce, grated cheese, and round slices of hard-cooked eggs. Follow same procedure until all ingredients are used, having rounds of eggs for last layer. Cover with remaining sauce. Bake in 350°F. oven 30 minutes. This will freeze. Serves 6.

MENUDO

(Tripe Soup)

This dish, which is a soup or stew, is considered a great restorative in Mexico, having a very salubrious effect on those who have celebrated too well the night before.

2 calves' feet (or a knuckle of veal)
6 quarts water
5 pounds tripe
3 cups hominy (nixtamal or canned whole hominy)

3 onions, minced
4 cloves garlic, minced
1 tablespoon orégano
2 teaspoons cilantro (coriander) seeds
Salt and pepper

Wash calves' feet and cook in water for 1 hour. (If veal knuckle is used, add with tripe.) Wash tripe, cut in pieces about 1 × 2 inches, and add to calves' feet. Add hominy, onion, and garlic. (If canned hominy is used, add during last hour of cooking.) Tie spices loosely in a cheesecloth bag and add. Simmer 6 or 7 hours, or until tripe is very tender. Serve this dish with chopped green onions and chopped fresh mint leaves, also with Mexican red chile sauce, if you wish. Serves 12.

GAZPACHO

I just never did care for Gazpacho, a popular cold soup in Spain,
and wouldn't you know that Helen Evans Brown served it one time
I was at her home for dinner. Much to my surprise, I was crazy
about it! She calls her recipe (which is in her *West Coast Cook
Book*) a West Coast version. The Spanish include layers of toast
or bread and that's one of the reasons I didn't like this summer
soup until Helen converted me.

1 clove garlic	2 cups tomato juice or ice
3 pounds tomatoes, very ripe	water
2 medium-sized cucumbers,	⅓ cup olive oil
peeled and chopped	3 tablespoons vinegar
½ cup minced green pepper	Salt and pepper
½ cup minced onion	Dash of Tabasco or 1 small
	hot red pepper

Rub a large bowl with a cut clove of garlic. Peel tomatoes, remove cores, and chop them in rather small pieces. Don't lose any
of that precious juice—pour it and the tomatoes into the bowl. Add
prepared cucumbers along with green pepper and onion, and tomato juice or ice water. Then add olive oil, vinegar, plenty of salt
and pepper (taste it!), and either the Tabasco or a fresh hot red
pepper minced into infinitesimal pieces. Chill very thoroughly; serve
with an ice cube in each dish. Serves 10 or 12.

SOPA DE FLAN

(Flan Soup)

Flan, as you'll find out in the dessert section, is a lovely Mexican
custard. I don't know how it got to be a soup, but I'm glad it did,

because this recipe from Mexico City is not just unusual, it's unusually good.

1½ quarts rich chicken broth	Salt and pepper
⅓ cup butter	
⅓ cup flour	Flan:
1 cooked breast of chicken, cubed	4 eggs
1 tablespoon minced parsley	¾ cup milk
1 cup rich cream	Salt and pepper

Melt butter, add flour, stirring to blend. When it starts to brown, add broth, chicken, parsley, salt, pepper, and flan, cut in small cubes. When ready to serve, add cream.

Flan: beat eggs, add milk, salt and pepper. Pour into a buttered casserole and bake in a pan of hot water at 325°F. for 25 minutes, or until firm. Serves 6 to 8.

Huevos

℘ (Eggs)

The Mexicans have more imagination than we do when it comes to cooking eggs. Some of their dishes are inherited from the Spanish, some are strictly their own, all are good. Probably the most famous one in the United States is *huevos rancheros,* at least the most famous one after that internationally known one, Spanish omelet.

TORTILLA DE HUEVO Y CHILE VERDE

(Green Chile and Cheese Omelet)

Green chile and cheese, that superlative combination of flavors, contributes to this dish that is especially well suited for a lazy-time breakfast or brunch. It's fine for luncheon or supper, too.

1 tablespoon butter	1 can peeled green chiles
4 eggs	¼ pound Monterey Jack or
4 tablespoons milk or cream	sharp Cheddar cheese,
Salt and pepper	cut in strips

Melt butter in heavy skillet. Beat together eggs, milk or cream, salt and pepper. Make omelet as usual, keeping it moist. Wrap chiles around each cheese strip and place on one half of omelet. Fold over and serve on heated platter. Serves 2 or 4.

For extra personality and glamour, serve with the following sauce:

1 tablespoon butter	1 tablespoon minced onion
1 large fresh tomato, peeled and chopped	

Melt butter; add remaining ingredients and simmer about 5 minutes. Pour over omelet just before serving.

HUEVOS REVUELTOS A LA MEXICANA

(Mexican Scrambled Eggs)

Mexicans do interesting things with eggs just as their former conquerors, the Spanish, do. Hot or toasted tortillas are especially good with them, and *that* the Mexicans learned from the Aztecs.

1 small tomato	1 tablespoon minced parsley
4 eggs	1 small green onion, finely
1 tablespoon milk	chopped
1 tablespoon minced green pepper	Salt and pepper

Peel tomato, remove seeds and cut in very small cubes. Beat

eggs, add milk and all other ingredients. Scramble in butter in the usual way. Serves 2.

CHORIZO CON HUEVOS

(Mexican Sausage with Eggs)

If you can't buy chorizos, make them. My recipe is on page 89.

3 ounces chorizo (Mexican sausage) for each person served

1 teaspoon oil for each chorizo
2 eggs for each chorizo

Remove skins from chorizos, crumble into hot oil and fry. Beat eggs, add to chorizo. Stir with a fork as you would scrambled eggs. For added flavor, stir in 1 tablespoon of minced onion or chopped green onions before eggs set.

HUEVOS RANCHEROS

(Eggs, Ranch Style)

A Mexican classic, this, as you'll find out when you take a trip to my native land. These eggs are usually served on tostadas, and refried beans accompany them, even at breakfast! Garnish with avocado slices and you'll have a meal!

2 tablespoons oil
1 tablespoon minced onion
1 small clove garlic, peeled
½ teaspoon orégano

1 or 2 chile tepines,* mashed and strained
1 (8 oz.) can tomato sauce
Salt
4 eggs

* Green peeled chiles or salsa Jalapeña may be used instead of chile tepines.

Wilt onion in oil, add garlic, orégano, chiles, tomato sauce, and salt. Simmer a few minutes. Poach eggs in the sauce or fry them separately and pour sauce over them. Serves 4.

HUEVOS RANCHEROS CALIFORNIANOS

(Ranch Eggs, California Style)

This will serve 3 two-egg eaters or 6 "one-eggers." They have a really robust flavor all their own.

2 tablespoons bacon drippings	¼ pound sharp Cheddar
2 tablespoons minced onion	cheese, cubed
1 can peeled green chiles	6 eggs
1 (No. 2) can solid-pack	Salt
tomatoes	

Wilt onion in bacon drippings, add chiles and tomatoes and simmer until almost dry. Add cheese. When it is almost melted, drop in whole eggs, one at a time, cooking to individual tastes.

TORTILLA CON HUEVOS

(Tortilla with Eggs)

Here's another superlative way with eggs. Just try *this* on your skillet!

1 tortilla	1 tablespoon grated Parmesan
3 tablespoons oil	cheese
2 eggs, well beaten	Salt and pepper
2 tablespoons milk	

Cut tortilla into eighths and fry in hot oil (but not too crisp, please!). Combine eggs, milk, cheese, salt and pepper and pour over fried tortilla. Cook as you would any French or plain omelet. Serves 1 or 2.

TORTILLA DE HUEVO A LA ESPAÑOLA

(Spanish Omelet)

Don't be confused by this. In Spain an omelet is called a *tortilla;* in Mexico an omelet is a *tortilla de huevo* (egg tortilla). And you know what the other kind is!

3 tablespoons oil	*2 (8 oz.) cans tomato sauce*
1 small onion, minced	*Salt and pepper*
1 green pepper, chopped fine	

Make sauce by wilting onion and green pepper in hot oil. Add tomato sauce, salt and pepper and simmer for 20 minutes. Prepare four individual omelets, using 2 eggs and 2 tablespoons milk for each. Serve omelets on hot platter, topped with sauce. If desired, season the sauce with a little chile powder.

HUEVOS POBLANOS

(Eggs, Pueblo Style)

Here's a wonderful dish for a hungry crowd. It's simple to prepare and outstanding in flavor—so everyone says.

1 can peeled green chiles	*6 eggs*
1½ cups light cream	*½ cup grated Swiss cheese*
Salt	

Whirl chiles and cream in electric blender. Add salt and pour into a buttered shallow baking dish. Break eggs on top of sauce, sprinkle with cheese and bake at 350°F. for 10 minutes, or until eggs are set. Serves 3 to 6.

HUEVOS A LA NAVARRA

(Eggs, Navarra Style)

Easy, this—and delicious. Cecilia Donahue, from Havana, Cuba, whom I have known since she was a small child, gave me this recipe.

1 tablespoon butter	*8 eggs*
3 medium-sized tomatoes,	*¼ pound longaniza sausage*
peeled and chopped	*1 tablespoon grated*
2 tablespoons chopped parsley	*Parmesan or Romano*
Salt and pepper	*cheese*

Generously butter a shallow baking dish. Mix tomatoes with parsley, salt and pepper and put a layer of them at the bottom of the dish. Break eggs on top and place rounds of longaniza around the yolks. Sprinkle with grated cheese and bake at 375°F. until eggs are set. Serves 4 or 8.

CHILAQUILES DE HUEVO

(Tortilla Hash)

Try this on your brunch table. If you want them spicier, add some Mexican chile sauce, but as for me I'll take them as is.

6 tortillas, cut in eighths
2 tablespoons butter or
    margarine
2 tablespoons minced onion
2 medium-sized tomatoes,
    peeled and cubed

3 eggs, beaten
Salt and pepper
1 tablespoon grated Parmesan
    cheese

Fry tortillas lightly in butter; add onion and tomatoes and fry until onion is limp. Then quickly add eggs, salt and pepper. Stir with a fork, as you would scrambled eggs, and cook until eggs are of desired consistency. Sprinkle with cheese and serve at once. Serves 4.

SUGGESTIONS FOR EGGS

When serving eggs for a group, a nice idea is to arrange varied omelets on a hot platter. One omelet may be made with tomato sauce, another with any green vegetable added, and one plain. Alternate them to give a tri-color effect, like the Mexican flag. Also, an omelet made with fried rings of onion is delightful.

Pescados

⅌ (Fish)

Mexico, having as it does much coastline, also has many wonderful fish and shellfish. The most famous Mexican fish dishes are *escabeche* and *seviche,* but many other wonderful things are done with them—such as adding them to rice, for *paella* and *sopas secas.*

ARROZ DE VIGILIA CON JAIBA
(Lenten Crab and Rice)

3 tablespoons butter or margarine

2 cups uncooked rice

1 bunch green onions, chopped

2 tomatoes, peeled and chopped

1 clove garlic, mashed or pressed

2 tablespoons minced parsley

2 peeled green chiles, chopped

¼ cup finely chopped celery

1 pound crab legs, shrimp or lobster

4½ cups water

Salt and pepper

Fry rice lightly in butter in large kettle. Add all other ingredients and simmer for 30 minutes, or until all liquid has been absorbed. Serves 6 to 8.

RISOLES DE CAMARONES, MARJORIE

(Marjorie's Shrimp Fritters)

Everyone seems to like these little fritters of mine. They are good as appetizers, too, made the same way but much smaller. I have named them for Marjorie Lumm of the Wine Institute, who has been of very great help in the preparation of this book.

½ cup water	½ cup grated American cheese
2 tablespoons butter or margarine	1 cup cooked shrimp or 1 (5 oz.) can shrimp, drained
½ cup sifted flour	Lemon wedges
2 eggs	Paprika

Bring water and butter to a boil in a saucepan, add flour, stirring vigorously until mixture forms a ball and leaves the sides of the pan. Remove from heat and add eggs, one at a time, beating well after each addition. Beat until batter is smooth and thick, then stir in cheese and shrimps. Drop mixture by small spoonfuls into heated shallow fat, fry on both sides until browned. Drain on absorbent paper and serve, allowing 2 per serving. Makes 12. Garnish with lemon wedges and a sprinkling of paprika.

ATÚN EN ESCABECHE

(Pickled Tuna Fish)

Fresh tuna, common in Mexico and on the Pacific coast, makes a particularly good *escabeche*. It is a refreshing dish nice to include at a summer buffet.

5 pounds tuna fish, sliced	4 bay leaves
2 cups oil	1 tablespoon whole black
3 large onions, cut in rings	pepper
5 cloves garlic	Salt to taste
1 pint vinegar	

Salt slices of fish, remove dark meat, and fry until brown in the oil. Place in a crockery jar or earthenware casserole in layers. When all the fish has been fried, fry onions and garlic in the same oil about 5 minutes. Add vinegar, bay leaves, and whole pepper, heat to boiling and pour at once over fish. If fish is not well covered, add more vinegar. This fish should not be eaten until at least 24 hours after it is made, for the flavor improves as time goes on.

ESCABECHE DE PESCADO

(Soused or Pickled Fish)

This recipe is another from Helen Brown's *West Coast Cook Book,* published by Little, Brown and Company.

2 pounds fish fillets	2 tablespoons slivered orange
Butter	zest
½ cup olive or salad oil	2 tablespoons slivered green
2 tablespoons vinegar	pepper
¼ cup orange juice	2 tablespoons minced green
2 teaspoons salt	onion
¼ teaspoon cayenne	Orange slices

Lightly brown fillets of any small fish in a little butter and arrange them carefully in a flat dish, keeping them whole. Make a sauce with oil, vinegar, orange juice, zest of orange (the very outside, orange part of the skin) cut in tiny slivers, green pepper cut in the same size pieces as the orange, and the minced green onion or shallots. Pour over the fish and let stand in the refrigerator for 6 or 8 hours, or longer, basting the fish with the sauce once or twice. At the same time, chill thick slices of unpeeled orange in French dressing, and garnish the finished dish with them. Serves 6.

BACALAO A LA VIZCAINA

(Codfish Spanish Style)

Some of Mexico's finest dishes show their Spanish heritage. This one, using the lowly salt cod, has real glamour.

1 pound salted codfish	2 cloves garlic, minced
1 large onion, minced	1 can pimientos
½ cup olive oil	2 tablespoons parsley, minced
3 large fresh tomatoes, or 2 cups solid-pack tomatoes	Salt and pepper
	1 small jar stuffed olives, sliced

Soak codfish overnight in cold water to cover. Drain and shred. Wilt onion in oil, add codfish and cook a few minutes. Add tomatoes, garlic, pimientos, parsley, salt, pepper, and olives. Simmer slowly until codfish is tender. Serves 4.

PESCADO FRIO EN SALSA DE PIÑÓN

(Cold Fish in Pine Nut Sauce)

A lovely dish for a warm summer day. Pine nuts are expensive but a few go a long way and their delicate flavor can't be equaled.

2 to 2½ pounds halibut (in one piece)
Salt and pepper
Juice of one lemon
1 medium-sized onion, sliced
2 tablespoons olive oil
¼ pound cooked shrimps, chopped

Pine nut sauce (page 169)
1 cup cooked cubed carrots
1 cup cooked cubed potatoes
1 cup cooked string beans, cut in small pieces
Oil, wine vinegar, salt, and pepper
Lemon wedges

Wipe fish with paper towel and rub all over with salt, pepper, and lemon juice. Place in a shallow baking dish, add onion, pour oil over it and bake at 350°F. until fish flakes easily with a fork, about 40 to 45 minutes. When fish is cold, place on a large platter, split to remove bones, spread half with a mixture of chopped shrimps and half of the pine nut sauce. Put other half of fish on top, spread remaining sauce over it. Add oil, vinegar, salt and pepper to the vegetables and put in little separate mounds all around the fish. Garnish with lemon wedges. Serves 6 to 8.

PESCADO RELLENO CON CAMARÓN

(Fish Stuffed with Shrimp)

Let this cold fish dish star at a summer buffet.

2 large fillets of rock cod or
    similar white fish
1 medium-sized onion, sliced
1 clove garlic

1 bay leaf
1 teaspoon orégano
Salt and pepper

Stuffing:

½ cup butter
 1 medium-sized onion,
    minced
⅓ cup sifted flour
 2 cups milk

¼ pound cooked shrimps,
    coarsely chopped
Mayonnaise, pimientos,
    hard-cooked egg, and
    lettuce

Simmer fish in water to cover, with onion, garlic, bay leaf, orégano, salt and pepper, until fish separates easily when tested with a fork. Drain and allow to cool. Set aside. For the stuffing, melt butter, add onion, blend in flour; add milk and cook, stirring until smooth and thick. Add shrimps and cool. Place one fillet on serving platter, spread filling over it, then cover with the other fillet. Chill in refrigerator for about 2 hours. Before serving, cover with mayonnaise. Garnish with strips of pimiento, slices of hard-cooked egg, and lettuce or parsley. If you prefer, striped bass is very good. Leave the head and tail on and decorate the platter so that it looks like a live fish, using olives for the eyes. Serves 4 to 6.

ARROZ CON ALMEJAS

(Rice with Clams)

In Mexico, as in Spain (particularly near the Bay of Biscay where there are many Basques), this dish is highly regarded. The clams are used whole and in their shells, but if you wish you may substitute canned clams, shucked, or not.

¼ cup olive oil	2 pounds small clams, in the
1 medium-sized onion,	shell
chopped	5 cups clam broth or nectar
2 cloves garlic, minced	2 cups uncooked rice
1 teaspoon paprika	Salt and pepper to taste
2 tablespoons minced parsley	

Wilt onion in oil, add garlic, paprika, and parsley. Scrub clams well, put in a covered pot with ½ cup water, and steam until the clams open. Reserve clams. Strain juice through double cheese-cloth, add enough water to make the desired amount, and add onion mixture, along with rice and salt and pepper. Cover and simmer for 30 minutes, or until all the liquid is absorbed, adding clams the last 5 minutes of cooking. If canned clams are used, add water or clam nectar to juices to make the desired amount of liquid. Two 10-ounce cans of clams will suffice. Serves 6 to 8.

PESCADO A LA VERACRUZANA

(Fish, Veracruz Style)

This is a classic Mexican dish, but in that country they use *huachinango*. It's easy to fix, and easy to take, my friends say. Even if you don't like fish, you'll like this.

2 pounds red snapper
Olive oil (about ¼ cup)
1 large onion, chopped
1 (No. 2½) can solid-pack
tomatoes, chopped

1 can pimientos, coarsely
chopped
2 tablespoons capers
1 (3 oz.) jar green olives
Salt and pepper

Wilt onion in olive oil; add tomatoes, salt and pepper and cook about 5 minutes to blend flavors. Place red snapper in buttered baking dish; add pimientos, capers, and olives; pour tomato sauce over and bake at 350°F. for 25 to 30 minutes or until fish flakes easily with a fork. Serves 6.

ARROZ CON BACALAO

(Rice with Codfish)

Codfish, a favorite in Spain, is quite naturally well liked in Mexico.

1 pound salt codfish, in one
piece
2 onions, sliced
3 leeks
2 cloves garlic
4½ cups fish stock*
¼ cup olive oil
2 cups uncooked rice

1 onion, chopped
3 fresh tomatoes, peeled and
chopped, or 1½ cups
solid-pack tomatoes
1 bay leaf
Pinch of nutmeg
Salt and pepper

Cook fish in water (about 6 cups) with onion slices, leeks, and garlic. When tender, strain, saving the stock, and shred codfish. Fry rice lightly in oil with chopped onion, add tomatoes, stock, codfish, bay leaf, nutmeg, salt and pepper. Cover and simmer for about 30 minutes. Serves 8 to 10.

* Add water, if necessary, to make required amount of liquid.

ARROZ A LA CUBANA

(Rice, Cuban Style)

Good for Fridays and many other days. I especially like it with large shrimps, but it's mighty fine with crab meat or lobster, if you want a change.

4 tablespoons olive oil	½ cup tomato sauce
3 cloves garlic	1 cup white table wine
1 medium-sized onion, chopped	3 cups chicken broth
1 medium-sized green pepper, coarsely chopped	½ teaspoon black pepper, coarsely ground
1 pound uncooked large shrimps, cut in pieces	2 cups uncooked rice
	Salt
	Grated Parmesan cheese

Fry garlic in oil for a few minutes. Remove garlic; to the oil add onion, green pepper, and shrimps. Fry until shrimps turn light pink; add tomato sauce, wine, chicken broth, and black pepper. When it comes to a boil, add rice, stir well. Then cover and simmer for about 30 minutes, or until all liquid has been absorbed. Just before serving, sprinkle with cheese. Serves 4 to 6.

TORTAS DE CAMARÓN

(Shrimp Fritters, Mexican Style)

This is a must for Lent. The Mexicans use dried shrimps only, but I prefer the combination. If you wish, substitute 1 cup cooked fresh shrimps plus ¼ cup of water in which they were cooked.

1 can wet pack shrimps (save   4 eggs, separated
    liquid)   2 tablespoons flour
¾ cup dried shrimps (buy at a
    Mexican store)

Chop canned shrimps, add dried shrimps, and mix well. Beat whites of eggs stiff but not dry; beat egg yolks lightly and fold into whites, then fold in the flour. Add chopped shrimps to this batter. Drop by spoonfuls into moderately hot oil or shortening about 1½ inches deep, and fry brown on both sides; remove to absorbent paper to drain.

Now make sauce as follows:

2 tablespoons oil   Liquid from canned shrimps
2 tablespoons minced onion   1 (8 oz.) bottle red chile sauce
1 clove garlic   (from a Mexican store)

Fry the onion and garlic in the oil. Add shrimp liquid and red chile sauce. Season, being careful not to add too much salt for shrimps are salty in themselves. About 5 minutes before serving, drop fritters into this sauce and heat through for a few minutes. If desired, cactus plant (*nopales*) may be used with these fritters. Just drain, wash, and redrain the canned nopales, and heat them in the sauce with the fritters. If the sauce is too hot with chile for you, dilute with water to suit your taste. Serves 6.

Pollos y Aves

ℰ (Chicken and Poultry)

Chicken is a great favorite in Mexico, as it is almost anywhere in the world. Some of the most famous dishes, like *Arroz con Pollo,* feature it, and it is often used in conjunction with other ingredients. Turkey is best known in the great party and fiesta dish, *Mole de Guajolote.*

GUAJOLOTE CON CASTAÑAS

(Turkey with Chestnuts)

Mama used to make this turkey for New Year's. My younger and favorite brother, Manuel Loshuertos, looked forward to that day because he knew the treat in store for him.

Stuffing for a 16-pound turkey:

3 pounds chestnuts	Salt and pepper
1 pound butter	Nutmeg
12 cups bread cubes	White wine or cream

To shell chestnuts, boil for ten minutes, then remove from hot water one at a time, and remove outer and inner shell. It doesn't matter if the chestnuts break. When all are shelled, cook until tender in turkey stock made from neck and giblets (use remaining stock). This will take another 10 or 15 minutes.

Crisp bread cubes in butter, add chestnuts (not chopped), cook a couple of minutes, then season to taste with salt, pepper, and freshly grated nutmeg. Add just enough white wine or cream to moisten slightly.

Stuff turkey; roast in your favorite manner.

GUAJOLOTE RELLENO A LA MEXICANA

(Stuffed Turkey, Mexican Style)

1 16-pound turkey	½ pound prunes, soaked and
10 apples, peeled and	pitted
quartered	½ cup blanched almonds
2 cups sherry	Salt, pepper, and nutmeg to
½ pound butter	taste
½ of a pound cake or butter	
cake, crumbled	

Cook apples slightly in the sherry. Melt butter, add to apples along with all other ingredients. Season to taste, stuff and roast turkey as usual.

MOLE DE GUAJOLOTE

(Mole Sauce for Turkey)

This recipe, created by Helen Evans Brown, is used by courtesy of *McCall's* magazine. I wish to thank them.

The classic Mexican method of making a mole consists of laborious hours of scraping pulp from several different kinds of chiles, and grinding nuts and seeds and chocolate in a mortar. The recipe below is a very modern version which nonetheless has the authentic Mexican flavor.

1 small turkey (about 12 pounds)	4 tablespoons toasted sesame seeds
2 chopped onions	2 teaspoons ground cumin
3 large cloves garlic, minced	¾ cup chile powder
4 tablespoons lard or turkey fat	4 dried tortillas, or ½ cup corn meal
4 squares bitter chocolate	2½ tablespoons sugar
1 cup peanut butter	¼ teaspoon anise
6 cups turkey stock	Salt to taste

Have turkey cut in pieces, cover with water, and simmer until just tender, adding salt to taste. In the meantime, cook the chopped onion and garlic in the shortening until wilted, and put in a blender along with the chocolate, cut in pieces, 1 cup of the stock, and the remaining ingredients. (Toast sesame seeds in a heavy dry skillet, stirring so that they won't burn. Break tortillas in pieces; if not dry, put them in a slow oven until hard.) Blend ingredients until smooth, adding remaining stock and more salt if necessary; then pour over the drained turkey pieces. If you have no blender, grind the dry ingredients several times, using the finest knife, then mix with the stock. Heat thoroughly before serving. (This improves if made the day before serving.) Serves 12.

POLLO DESHUESADO

(Boned Chicken)

Don't tell me that these are too hard to do. If I can do them, so can you! Actually, I do have them often, as they are one of my favorite "company" dishes. I hope my guests like them as well as they say they do.

Order small young chickens and ask your butcher to remove necks and wing tips. Cut the skin down the back and remove the bones with a sharp paring knife, scraping the chicken off the skeleton until only the lower leg bone and upper wing are left. I usually stuff the chickens with the recipe I give here, but picadillo (page 88) makes a delicious and unusual stuffing. The stuffing recipe given here is for 6 chickens. The picadillo recipe will stuff about 3.

¼ *pound butter*
1 *medium-sized onion,*
  chopped fine
1 *mashed clove of garlic*
½ *pound raw ham, cut in small*
  dice (don't remove fat!)
½ *pound fresh mushrooms*

2 *large French rolls, cut in*
  small pieces
Salt and pepper to taste
¼ *cup half and half (cream and*
  milk), or white table
  wine

Cook onions and garlic in butter until wilted, add ham, then chopped mushroom stems, saving the caps to garnish the chickens. Cook until mushrooms are tender, then add bread cubes. (This makes them quite juicy.) Season to taste, and mix in the half and half or table wine. Stuff the chickens, filling up hollows and shaping with hands. Rub the birds with butter or oil, and roast at 325°F. until tender. Serve chickens whole and split them at table with poultry shears, allowing ½ chicken per person.

JESSICA'S POLLOS ELEGANTES

(Jessica's Elegant Chickens)

Without my darling friend, Jessica McLachlin Greengard, this book could not have been written. Although her life is full of helping others, she always makes time for me. My heart is full of gratitude.

This is my idea of a good, easy recipe to serve to a crowd. Allow a half chicken for each person and you'll have more than enough. Which is the way I like it.

2 chickens (2 to 2½ pounds each, ready-to-cook weight) split in halves	4 strips bacon, cut crosswise in halves
4 tablespoons soft butter or margarine	2 cups California sauterne
Salt and pepper	1 cup chicken stock
	½ cup thinly sliced green onions
	¼ cup chopped parsley

Rub skin side of chicken halves with butter; sprinkle all over with salt and pepper. Place skin side down in a shallow baking pan; lay 2 half-strips of bacon on each piece; bake in a 425°F. oven 15 minutes. Mix remaining ingredients; pour over chicken; continue baking for 30 minutes, basting several times. Reduce heat to 350°F. Turn chicken skin side up, and continue baking and basting for 15 minutes, or until chicken is golden brown and tender. Serve with rice or triangles of toast, so that none of the good juices will be wasted. Serves 4 generously.

POLLO EN JUGO DE NARANJA

(Chicken in Orange Juice)

This chicken dish is as good to look at as it is to eat. It makes a hit with my boys every time. Try it on the men in your life.

1 frying chicken, disjointed	½ cup blanched ground
Seasoned flour	almonds
Oil for frying	½ cup crushed pineapple
1 cup orange juice	2 tablespoons sugar
1 cup white table wine	¼ teaspoon cinnamon
½ cup raisins	⅛ teaspoon cloves

Dredge chicken with seasoned flour. Brown in oil. Place chicken in shallow glass baking dish. Combine all other ingredients and pour over chicken. Bake at 325°F. basting often, for 30 minutes. Raise temperature to 350°F. and bake 15 minutes longer. Serves 3 or 4.

POLLO ESTILO MAZATLÁN

(Chicken, Mazatlán Style)

On one of my trips to Mazatlán, I was introduced to this dish. There it is served at umbrella-shaded tables in the open-air markets, or plazas, as they are called. Refried beans and hot tortillas were served with it, making a memorable meal.

1 cooked fricassee chicken, cut in pieces
Oil for frying
2 large potatoes boiled in jackets, peeled and sliced
1 cup cooked string beans, cut in pieces
3 large zucchini, cooked with

water and 1 tablespoon vinegar
Shredded lettuce
Salt and pepper
Tostada and taco sauce #2 (page 166)
1 avocado, cut in wedges
Radish rosettes

Fry cooked chicken in oil until brown. Set aside and keep warm. Brown potatoes in the same oil, set aside and keep warm. Serve individually by arranging a layer each of chicken, potatoes, string beans, zucchini and lettuce. Pour sauce, as much or as little as you wish, over all. The sauce may be served hot or cold. Garnish with radish rosettes in the center of each serving and avocado on the side. Serves 6.

PECHUGAS DE REY

(Chicken Breasts Fit for a King)

Here's a fancy dish that can be fixed in the shake of a hen's tail—especially if you have some chicken breasts in your freezer.

This is a favorite with Spaniards, but you don't have to be Spanish to enjoy it.

4 breasts of chicken, cooked   *1 cup (¼ pound) coarsely*
1 (4 oz.) can pimientos, sieved   *grated Swiss cheese*
1 (14½ oz.) can evaporated   *Salt and pepper*
   milk   *Parsley sprigs*

Remove bones from chicken breasts (try to keep them in one piece!) and place them in a well-buttered shallow baking dish. Set aside. Combine pimientos, milk, salt, and pepper. Mix well and pour over chicken breasts. Sprinkle cheese over all and bake at 325°F. for 15 to 20 minutes, basting a couple of times. Garnish with parsley and serve with white rice or toast. Serves 4.

RELLENO DE NARANJA PARA POLLO

(Orange Stuffing for Chicken)

Here, again, the flavor of oranges does wonderful things for chicken, turkey, or duck.

3 cups toasted bread cubes   *1½ cups chopped celery*
½ cup orange juice   *½ cup finely chopped onion*
½ teaspoon grated orange   *½ cup chopped parsley*
   rind   *¼ cup butter or margarine*

Combine all ingredients in a large mixing bowl. Turn stuffing into a greased baking dish and bake in a 350°F. oven for 45 minutes, or stuff your bird with it and bake in the usual manner. Makes about 4 cups of stuffing.

POLLO EN CAMISA

(Chicken with a Shirt)

This is a chicken all dressed up.

2 small fryers, cut into
    serving-size pieces
2 tablespoons
    finely-chopped parsley
1 teaspoon thyme

1 teaspoon chile powder
Garlic salt and pepper to
    taste
Juice of one lemon

Batter:

1 egg
¾ cup water
1½ cups sifted flour
½ teaspoon salt

1 teaspoon baking soda
1 teaspoon thyme
1 tablespoon
    finely-chopped parsley

Sauce:

2 cups tomato purée or sour
    cream
1 clove garlic, mashed

1 can pimientos, cut in strips
Salt and pepper to taste

Season pieces of chicken with parsley, thyme, chile powder, garlic salt, pepper, and lemon juice. Allow to stand for one hour. Prepare batter by beating together until smooth and moderately thick, the egg, water, flour, salt, soda, thyme, and parsley. Dip the chicken, one piece at a time, in the batter, so that the pieces are completely covered. Drop into hot deep fat, cook until chicken is tender and the crust a deep, golden brown. Drain on absorbent paper and serve with the sauce, made by stirring all the sauce ingredients together in a saucepan and simmering for about 15 to 20 minutes. Garnish with sprigs of watercress or parsley and lemon wedges. Serves 6 to 8.

CREPAS DE POLLO

(Pancakes with Chicken, Mexican Style)

Crepas, like their French cousins, *Crêpes,* are being used more and more. Here is one of my pet fillings, but you can vary them to suit yourself. The tacos fillings in this book may give you some ideas.

Pancakes:

3 large eggs
1¼ cups milk
1½ cups sifted flour

1 teaspoon salt
2 tablespoons melted butter

Filling:

2 cups chopped cooked
   chicken
2 tablespoons minced onion

2 tablespoons chopped raisins
2 tablespoons blanched
   chopped almonds

Sauce:

2 cups chipotle sauce
   (page 168)

1 pint sour cream
Grated cheese

Beat eggs, add milk; combine with flour and salt. Add butter and mix. Pour about ¼ cupful into a 7-inch buttered skillet, and tip and turn so that the batter runs in a thin layer over the bottom of the pan. When brown on bottom, turn and brown lightly on other side. Continue until all batter is used.

Combine all filling ingredients. Mix well and put 1 tablespoonful in each pancake. Roll, as you would a taco, and place, seam side down, in a buttered shallow baking dish. Pour sauce over all, and spoon sour cream over sauce. Sprinkle with cheese and bake at 325°F. for 15 to 20 minutes. Makes 16 or more pancakes.

MANCHA MANTELES

(Tablecloth Stainer)

The name of this recipe may seem quaint but it is an old Mexican classic, and highly esteemed. I suppose it would stain the tablecloth but I'd rather eat than spill it. In Mexico they use a special variety of firm banana, called *macho,* which is not easy to find here. I have, therefore, changed the recipe so that the usual bananas found in the States may be used by adding them at the last minute. The combination of flavors will intrigue your family and friends.

1 pound lean pork loin, cut in small cubes
1 roasting chicken, disjointed

Seasoned flour
2 tablespoons butter or margarine
2 tablespoons oil

Sauce:

1 tablespoon blanched almonds
1 teaspoon sesame seeds
1 medium-sized onion, chopped
1 medium-sized green pepper, chopped
1 (8 oz.) can tomato sauce
1 quart boiling water
1 tablespoon chile powder

¼ cup sugar
½ teaspoon cinnamon
3 whole cloves
1 bay leaf
1 medium-sized sweet potato, cut in large cubes
½ cup peeled and cubed apple
1 cup pineapple tidbits
Salt to taste
Sliced bananas (optional)

Brown pork in skillet, in a mixture of oil and butter. Remove to a large saucepan. Dredge chicken with seasoned flour and brown in the same drippings. Remove from skillet and add to pork. Slightly fry almonds and sesame seeds in the same fat, add onion and green pepper and fry a few minutes longer. Add tomato sauce and put through electric blender or food grinder. Blend this ground mixture with water, chile powder, sugar, cinnamon, cloves, bay leaf and salt. Cook for 10 to 15 minutes to blend flavors, and sieve. Pour this sauce over pork and chicken. Simmer for 30 minutes. Add sweet potatoes, simmer 15 minutes longer. Then put in the apple and pineapple and cook for a final few minutes, just long enough to blend.

Serve hot in soup plates, the bananas sliced right into the hot stew. Warm tortillas go nicely with this dish. Be sure to have enough paper napkins handy, or large cloth ones. Better still, provide your guests with bibs as this is really a "tablecloth stainer."

GALLINA EN PIPIÁN

(Chicken in Pipián Sauce)

This dish is well liked by Mexicans and by Americans who are lucky enough to have it. It is nice served with refried beans and with plenty of hot tortillas to "spoon up" the sauce.

6 to 8 chiles anchos	1 quart chicken broth
½ cup dry corn, toasted	½ cup lard or oil
1 cup pumpkin seeds, toasted,	Salt to taste
or pepitas	1 fricassee chicken, disjointed
½ cup peanuts	and cooked
2 cloves garlic	

Wash and dry chiles. Remove seeds and soak in hot water until tender. Combine chiles, using one cup of the water in which they were soaked, with corn, pumpkin seeds, peanuts, and garlic. Blend thoroughly using electric blender or the fine blade of food grinder. Add half of the broth to this mixture and sieve. Heat lard or oil, add sieved mixture and salt. Simmer until it begins to thicken. Add remaining broth and chicken. Cook for 10 to 15 minutes longer, or until chicken is well coated with sauce. Serves 4 to 6.

POLLO A LA BARCELONA

(Chicken, Barcelona Style)

My parents were married in Barcelona, in Spain, and lived there many years. This was one of my mother's favorite recipes.

1 frying chicken, disjointed	*½ cup pimiento-stuffed olives*
2 tablespoons butter	*¼ pound sautéed fresh*
2 tablespoons oil	*mushrooms*
3 tablespoons flour	*2 tablespoons minced onions*
2 cups broth	*Salt and pepper*
½ cup Burgundy or Claret	

Brown chicken in a mixture of butter and oil. Remove from oil, set aside. Add flour to the drippings and blend well. Pour in broth and wine and cook, stirring, until mixture boils and thickens. Add olives, mushrooms, onions, salt and pepper. Return chicken to sauce, cover and simmer for 45 minutes, or until tender, basting occasionally. Serves 4.

CASEROLA DE POLLO Y ELOTE
(Chicken and Corn Casserole)

Use chicken parts for this if you want to; legs, breasts, thighs, or wings. Fresh or frozen corn can be used, too—1½ cups of it —in place of the canned kind. If you want to make it a party dish, pipe the mashed potatoes on with a pastry bag and star tube. This makes a wonderful buffet dish.

1 fryer, disjointed	*1½ cups chicken broth*
¾ cup seasoned flour	*1 (12 oz.) can whole kernel*
Oil for frying	*corn*
3 tablespoons butter or	*1 can peeled green chiles,*
margarine	*chopped*
Flour remaining from	*Salt to taste*
dredging	*2 or 3 cups seasoned mashed*
1½ cups rich milk	*potatoes*

Dredge each piece of chicken thoroughly with seasoned flour and fry in hot oil until brown. Remove browned chicken to a large casserole. Set aside. Melt butter, add flour, milk and broth, blend well and bring to a boil. Add corn and chiles. Mix well and pour over chicken in casserole. Cover and bake at 350°F. until chicken is tender. Remove from oven, uncover and spoon mashed potatoes on top, filling in around edge of casserole. Brush with melted butter and bake for 15 minutes longer, or until potatoes are lightly browned. Serves 6 to 8.

MOLE DE GUAJOLOTE

(Mole Sauce for Turkey)

This is Mexico's great feast dish—served on state occasions and at fiestas. The story goes that some nuns in a lonely convent learned that they were to have a visit from a great church dignitary. Their larder was all but empty, but they rounded up what was to be found, killed their one and only turkey, and concocted this dish, using, as we'd say in America, "everything but the kitchen sink." Try it—it will be worth your time, believe me. If, however, you just don't have the time, use canned mole sauce or mole powder, available at Mexican food stores.

1 turkey, cooked and cut in pieces	1 2-inch stick cinnamon
	3 whole cloves
15 chiles mulatos	6 whole black peppercorns
15 chiles anchos	2 cloves garlic, peeled
5 chiles pasillas	1 (10 oz.) can tomatillo, drained
2 tablespoons mixed seeds from chiles	3 tomatoes, peeled
⅓ cup almonds	2 ounces Mexican chocolate
⅓ cup peanuts	2 quarts chicken broth
⅓ cup pumpkin seeds	1 teaspoon sugar
1 tortilla, fried crisp	Salt to taste
1 French roll, cut in half and fried crisp	½ cup lard
2 tablespoons sesame seeds	2 ounces sesame seeds, toasted (optional)

Wash and dry chiles. (They are all of different flavor and color and can be found at Mexican food stores, where you will find many of the other ingredients called for.) Toast chiles lightly in an ungreased skillet, remove seeds, and soak them in hot water to cover, until tender. Toast the chile seeds with the almonds, peanuts, and pumpkin seeds. Now put all the above ingredients, together with the tortilla, roll, sesame seeds, cinnamon, cloves, black peppercorns, garlic, tomatillo, tomatoes, and chocolate, through electric blender or food grinder. Add one quart of broth to ground mixture, mix well and strain. Heat lard, add strained sauce, sugar, and salt. Cook, stirring often, until sauce is thick. Add the remaining broth, the turkey, and heat thoroughly. When serving, sprinkle with the toasted sesame seeds, if desired. Serves 10 to 12.

POLLO CON JOCOQUI

(Chicken with Sour Cream)

Brides might well add this to their kitchen repertoire. It is easy to fix and never fails to make a hit. I serve it with noodles or rice and some very special dessert. My friends call it party chicken.

1 5-pound roasting chicken, cut in serving pieces	½ pound fresh mushrooms, sliced
Flour, salt and pepper	1 clove garlic, crushed
1 cup oil	2 tablespoons butter
¼ cup butter	½ cup sour cream
¼ cup rich chicken broth	½ cup heavy cream
1 small onion, chopped	Salt and pepper

Simmer chicken giblets and neck in water to make the broth. Rub the chicken pieces with the seasoned flour and brown in the oil, turning to color all sides. Butter a roasting pan generously, arrange the chicken in it, dot with butter, pour the broth over it and bake in a 350°F. oven until the chicken is tender. Cook the onion, mushrooms, and garlic in 2 tablespoons of butter until wilted, discard garlic, and add the sour and sweet cream and salt

and pepper to taste. Heat gently but do not boil. Arrange chicken
on a hot platter, pour sauce over it and serve with pride. Serves
6 to 8.

GUAJOLOTE EN MOLE VERDE

(Turkey in Green Mole Sauce)

You'll think you are in Mexico when you eat this heavenly dish.
I have made it mild, to suit most American palates, but there is
no reason for not adding chile relish to taste.

1 cooked small turkey,	*¼ cup blanched almonds*
disjointed	*1 can peeled green chiles*
1 (10 oz.) can tomatillo,	*2 cups rich chicken broth*
drained	*Salt to taste*
½ cup pumpkin seeds or	*¼ cup oil*
Pepitas	*½ cup minced parsley*

Put tomatillo, pumpkin seeds, almonds, and chiles through
blender or fine blade of food grinder. Mix broth with ground
mixture, add salt and simmer in hot oil for 10 minutes. Then
add turkey, cook 10 minutes longer, add parsley and cook 5
minutes longer before serving. Serves 8 to 10.

POLLO DE HACIENDA

(Chicken, Country Style)

Ah, the magic of the chile. Here is a simple chicken dish raised to epicurean heights by the addition of that chile!

6 to 8 pieces frying chicken
Oil
Flour seasoned with salt, pepper, and paprika
4 strips bacon, cut in small pieces
2 to 3 carrots, sliced

1 can peeled green chiles, cut in strips
1 tablespoon finely-chopped parsley
1 small bay leaf
1 small sprig thyme
1 lemon, thinly sliced
2 cups tomato juice

Dredge each piece of chicken thoroughly with seasoned flour. Fry in hot oil until golden brown. Remove browned chicken to a large casserole or baking dish. Add bacon, carrots, chiles, parsley, bay leaf, thyme, and any remaining seasoned flour. Place lemon slices on top of chicken and pour tomato juice over all. Cover casserole and bake in preheated 350°F. oven until chicken is tender—about 1 hour. Will freeze. Serves 6 to 8.

PASTEL DE POLLO A LA MEXICANA

(Chicken Pie, Mexican Style)

1 tablespoon butter or
  margarine
1 small onion, minced
1 pound tomatoes, peeled
  and chopped
  Salt and pepper
½ cup cooked peas, fresh or
  frozen

1 tablespoon chopped parsley
2 or more peeled green chiles,
  chopped
2 cups cubed, cooked white
  meat of chicken
  Standard recipe for pie crust
  (on the basis of 2 cups of
  flour)

Wilt onion in butter; add tomatoes, salt, and pepper; cook until thick. Add all other ingredients and mix well. Line a 9-inch pie plate with pastry. Spread filling on top. Cut a strip of pastry 2 inches wide and long enough to go around edge of pie. Dampen edge of lower crust and place this strip on top, around edge. Seal firmly. Center of pie should be open. Bake at 400°F. for 20 to 30 minutes or until nicely browned. Serves 4.

TAMAL DE POLLO Y ELOTE
(Chicken and Fresh Corn Tamale Pie)

It is a little trouble to prepare the corn in this manner, but the texture of the dough will reward your efforts. I prefer to use choice pieces of chicken rather than a whole one. This is a superb casserole dish.

3 tablespoons oil
1 frying chicken, disjointed, or chicken parts
2 cloves garlic, minced
2 medium-sized onions, chopped
2 medium-sized tomatoes, peeled and chopped, or 1½ cups solid-pack tomatoes

1 can peeled green chiles, chopped
½ teaspoon orégano, rubbed between the palms of hands
¼ teaspoon comino
Salsa Jalapeña, or your favorite chile relish, to taste
Salt

Top:

3 ears of fresh corn
2 tablespoons butter or margarine, melted

2 eggs, separated
Salt

Fry chicken in oil in large kettle, but do not brown. Add garlic, onion, tomatoes, chiles, orégano, comino, salsa, and salt. Cover and cook slowly for 15 minutes. Meanwhile, slightly grate the corn, just to break the skin of each grain, then, with a table knife, scrape all the pulp from the cob. Add to it the butter and egg yolks, slightly beaten. Beat egg whites until stiff but not dry, and fold into corn mixture. Place the chicken in a buttered 2-quart casserole, pour the corn mixture over the top and bake at 350°F. for 1 hour and 15 minutes. This will freeze. Serves 4.

CONEJO ENVINADO

(Rabbit in Wine Sauce)

2 rabbits, cut in serving-size
    pieces
Seasoned flour
Oil for frying
1 onion, minced
1 green pepper, chopped
2 cloves garlic, mashed or
    pressed
¼ cup chopped celery

¼ cup catsup
1 tablespoon chile powder
    (or more)
½ cup hot broth
1½ cups Burgundy
2 tablespoons chopped
    raisins
2 tablespoons chopped
    green olives

Dredge rabbit with seasoned flour. Brown in hot oil. Remove from pan. Drain off excess fat and in the same pan, fry onion, green pepper, garlic, and celery until soft but not browned. Add catsup, chile powder, dissolved in the broth, wine, and additional salt, if needed. Simmer for 10 minutes. Add rabbit and continue cooking until rabbit is tender—about 30 to 40 minutes; then add raisins and olives. Serves 6 to 8.

CONEJO A LA ESPAÑOLA

(Rabbit, Spanish Style)

I think that Spaniards cook rabbit particularly well. This dish, for instance, is nice for a guest dinner.

1 rabbit, cut in serving-size   *2 tomatoes, peeled and*
   pieces   *chopped*
   Salt and pepper   *1 bay leaf*
¼ cup oil   *1 cup white table wine*
1 clove garlic   *1 tablespoon vinegar*
1 onion, minced

Roll rabbit in seasoned flour. Heat oil, add garlic clove and fry. When well browned, discard garlic and transfer rabbit, along with remaining ingredients, to kettle with tight fitting cover. Simmer covered for 1 hour, or until tender. Serves 4 to 6.

Carnes

❦ (Meats)

Meat is not as plentiful in Mexico as it is here so that our southern neighbors have learned to make a little go a long way. Thus, though meat flavors many wonderful dishes, it is not often used alone, but rather combined with many other ingredients. This makes most Mexican meat dishes economical—a virtue when the food budget needs bolstering.

CARNE DE PUERCO CON CHILE VERDE

(Pork with Green Chile Sauce)

To make this extra exciting—if a bit harder to eat—Mexicans add 1-inch pieces of corn on the cob. You may also add more chile sauce if you wish. This dish, popular all over Mexico, makes a wonderful tamale filling, without the pieces of corn, of course.

2 pounds lean pork, cut in
  cubes
½ cup water
2 cloves garlic
  Salt and pepper
1 large onion, chopped
1 cup solid-pack tomatoes

1 teaspoon cilantro
  (coriander) seeds, crushed
  and soaked in 1 tablespoon
  hot water
1 can peeled green chiles,
  chopped or cut in strips

Cook meat with water, garlic, salt and pepper, until all water is absorbed. Discard garlic. Let meat fry in its own fat until it starts to brown. Add onion, cook a few minutes longer, add tomatoes, water drained from cilantro, chiles, and additional salt if needed. Cook, covered, for 30 minutes longer, or until pork is tender. Serves 4 to 6.

MONDONGO A LA ESPAÑOLA

(Tripe, Spanish Style)

My mother often cooked potatoes, peeled and cut in quarters, with the tripe, and always asked my father if he wanted it "with or without"—"*con o sin,*" as she'd say in Spanish.

3 pounds tripe
1 quart water
1 large onion, chopped
¼ cup olive oil
2 cloves garlic, mashed or
  pressed
3 cans tomato sauce

1 bay leaf
  Salt and pepper
  Tabasco sauce (optional)
1 can pimientos, cut in large
  pieces, or 1 small jar
  stuffed green olives

Wash and cut tripe in long strips. Simmer, covered, in salted water for 1 hour. While it's cooking, make the sauce: Wilt onion in oil, add garlic, tomato sauce, bay leaf, salt, pepper, and Tabasco sauce. Simmer, covered for 15 minutes. Drain tripe, add to sauce and cook, covered, until tender. If you want the tripe *"con,"* add potatoes during the last half hour of cooking. The pimientos or olives go in just before serving. Serves 8.

MONDONGO ELEGANTE

(Elegant Tripe)

Here's another tripe dish. Have you noticed how popular it has recently become? It's always been so in Spain, though, and this particular recipe is party fare there, and I hope, here.

1 pound tripe	1 bay leaf
2 pigs' feet, washed	1 sprig parsley
thoroughly	2 cloves garlic
1 quart water	8 peppercorns
1 large onion	Salt

Sauce:

2 tablespoons chopped	1 cup white table wine
onion	1 tablespoon capers, or
2 tablespoons olive oil	more if desired
1 (8 oz.) can tomato sauce	1 (3 oz.) jar pimiento-stuffed
¼ pound uncooked ham,	olives
chopped	

Place tripe, pigs' feet, water, onion, bay leaf, parsley, garlic, peppercorns, and salt in kettle. Cover and simmer until tender. Cool. Remove meat from broth, strain and reserve 2 cups of broth. Remove bones from pigs' feet. Coarsely chop pigs' feet and tripe. Set aside. Wilt onion in oil, add tomato sauce, cook for 5 minutes. Add broth, ham, tripe, and pigs' feet, and wine. Adjust seasoning, simmer a few minutes longer, then add capers and olives. Serves 4 to 6.

EASY TAMALE PIE

This isn't really a Mexican dish but I include it because it is a cousin, once removed, to the Mexican. Besides, it is inexpensive, easy to make, and delicious.

2 tablespoons oil
1 onion, chopped
1 pound ground beef
2 cups canned tomatoes
   (*No. 303 can*)
2 cups cream-style corn
   (*No. 303 can*)
1 cup milk

1 cup uncooked yellow
   cornmeal
1½ teaspoons salt
1½ tablespoons chile powder
½ cup ripe olives
½ pound Monterey Jack
   cheese

In a heavy skillet, heat oil and cook onion until soft. Add beef and cook until lightly browned. Stir in all remaining ingredients, except olives and cheese, mixing well. Add olives; cover pie with chunks of cheese. Cover and cook on top of stove over low heat, about 20 to 25 minutes. Makes 6 to 8 servings.

ALBÓNDIGAS EN SALSA DE ALMENDRA
(Meat Balls in Almond Sauce)

Mexicans are proud of their *albóndigas* and here is the reason why. For a variation, wedges of hard-cooked eggs or spoonfuls of grated raw carrot may be inserted in meat balls before cooking. This almond sauce may also be used for chicken, rabbit, or tongue.

Sauce:

3 tablespoons oil	2 tablespoons minced
½ cup almonds	onion
1 slice bread	¼ cup tomato sauce
1 clove garlic	1½ cups chicken broth
	Salt and pepper

Meat balls:

2 slices bread	1 egg
½ cup hot milk	1½ teaspoons salt
¾ pound ground beef	Pepper
¾ pound ground pork	

Fry almonds, bread and garlic in hot oil until browned. Remove from oil; cool and grind or blend to the consistency of paste. Dilute with a little broth. Set aside. Wilt onion in the same oil, add tomato sauce, remaining broth, salt and pepper. Simmer from 5 to 10 minutes. For the meat balls, soak bread in milk, drain, and combine with meats. Add egg, salt, and pepper and mix thoroughly. Roll into small balls and add to boiling sauce. Cook, covered, for 25 to 30 minutes. Add almond mixture during the last 10 minutes of cooking. Cubed potatoes may be added and

cooked with meat balls, if desired. Freezes beautifully. Serves
6 to 8.

SAFARANCHO

(Easy Pork and Rice Dish)

This recipe brings back memories of my childhood days. When-
ever we would bring home unexpected company, mother was never
upset. She would just say, "Don't worry, just run to the butcher
to get me some pork chops and I'll make *Safarancho*."

1 tablespoon oil
*4 loin pork chops, cut in
   half*
*1 medium-sized onion,
   chopped*
*1 medium-sized green
   pepper, coarsely
   chopped*

1 cup uncooked rice
⅓ cup catsup
*1 teaspoon Worcestershire
   sauce*
Salt and pepper
*2½ cups boiling water or
   broth*

Pour oil in bottom of skillet and arrange meat on it; add onion
and green pepper. Sprinkle on the rice; add catsup, Worcestershire sauce, salt, and pepper. Pour boiling water or broth over
all, cover, and simmer for 45 minutes. Allow to stand 15 minutes before serving. Serves 4.

ALBÓNDIGAS CON YERBA BUENA

(Good Herb Meat Balls)

My dear friend, Susana Whisman, has been my faithful helper. She has been my eyes during the writing of this book.

Incidentally, *Yerba Buena,* the "good herb," was the name given to San Francisco in its early days. As it is now my home, and has been for 49 years, I honor it as well as Susana in this recipe.

Sauce:

1 tablespoon oil or drippings	2 cans of tomato sauce
1 medium-sized onion, chopped	1 cup water or broth
	Salt and pepper

Meat balls:

1 pound ground beef	1 egg
½ pound ground pork	Salt and pepper
1 cup cooked rice	1 cup shelled peas
3 green onions, chopped	(optional)
1 tablespoon chopped mint leaves	2 hard-cooked eggs, cut in small pieces

Wilt onion in hot oil or drippings; add tomato sauce, water or broth, salt and pepper. Simmer for 10 to 15 minutes. For the meat balls: combine meats with rice; add green onion, mint leaves, egg, salt, and pepper. Mix thoroughly and shape into little balls, placing a small piece of hard-cooked egg in center of each. Add to boiling sauce, cover and simmer for 30 to 40 minutes. Add peas during the last 15 minutes of cooking, if you are using them. Serves 6 to 8.

PICADILLO

(Mexican Meat Hash)

This, I might say, is a sort of Mexican mincemeat, but it is used for many more things than our American pie filling—tamales, for instance, and empanadas, tacos, enchiladas, and many other wonderful things.

*1 pound lean ground beef
  or pork*
1 onion, chopped
*3 tablespoons oil (omit when
  using pork)*
*2 tomatoes, or 1 cup solid-
  pack canned tomatoes*
2 tablespoons vinegar
1 teaspoon sugar
1 teaspoon cinnamon

Pinch of ground cloves
*¼ teaspoon ground cumin
  (optional)*
1 teaspoon salt
*½ cup raisins plumped in ¼
  cup hot stock or water*
*Peeled green chiles or
  chile powder*
*½ cup slivered blanched
  almonds*

Brown meat and onion in heated oil. Add all other ingredients except almonds. Stir to blend, bring to a boil, reduce heat and simmer for 30 to 45 minutes. Stir in almonds. Will freeze.

ZANCAS DE CARNERO A LA ESPAÑOLA

(Spanish Lamb Shanks)

I am including this for my dear friend, Norma Young, of KHJ, Los Angeles. She adores lamb shanks!

4 lamb shanks
Flour
Salt and pepper
3 tablespoons bacon
   drippings or other fat

½ cup chopped onion
½ cup chopped celery
1 (8 oz.) can tomato sauce
½ cup Burgundy
1 bay leaf

Dredge lamb shanks with flour seasoned with salt and pepper. Heat bacon drippings in a large heavy skillet, and brown lamb shanks slowly on all sides in this. Add onion, celery, tomato sauce, wine, bay leaf and salt and pepper to taste. Cover and simmer for about 1½ hours, or until meat is very tender, turning and basting shanks occasionally. Serves 4.

CHORIZO A LA MEXICANA

(Mexican Sausage)

This is an important recipe as *chorizo* is used in many Mexican dishes but can't be found everywhere. When my recipes call for one chorizo, use about 3 ounces, or ⅓ of a cup.

1 pound lean pork
1 teaspoon salt
2 tablespoons chile powder
1 clove garlic, mashed or
   pressed

1 teaspoon orégano, rubbed
   between palms of hands
2 tablespoons vinegar

Grind coarsely or chop pork. Add all other ingredients and mix thoroughly. Let stand for several hours. Fry without adding fat for about 30 minutes. If you aren't going to use immediately, pack the uncooked chorizo in a crock or glass jar and keep in the refrigerator. It will keep for several weeks.

COSTILLAS DE PUERCO

(Spareribs)

Sparerib lovers take notice! Here they are at their best—crispy and tender with nothing to hide that succulent pork flavor. Here's where my younger son Bill comes in, and very quickly too when spareribs are for dinner. He finds them as irresistible as I find his good nature and teasing.

This is so simple that I see no reason for even listing the ingredients. Just cut each rib separately, sprinkle with salt and pepper, and put in a 300°F. oven. Every now and then, drain the fat and toss the ribs around. That's all I do. Drain constantly, allow to brown, never raising the temperature. This takes from 1½ to 2 hours. Serve these with *salsa fria*.

CECINA EN MOLE ESTILO TOLUCA

(Corned Beef in Mole Sauce)

Corned beef and zucchini—that's a switch but a good one. I like to serve this dish with hot tortillas and refried beans.

4 to 5 pounds corned beef
　(in one piece)
Cold water to cover
1 medium-sized onion
1 bay leaf
1 orange, cut in half
　Half a lemon

2 cloves garlic, mashed or
　pressed
2 or more tablespoons chile
　powder
⅛ teaspoon cumin powder
1 pound zucchini, cut in large
　pieces

Place corned beef in large kettle, add water, onion, bay leaf, orange, and lemon. Cover and simmer until tender. Combine garlic, chile powder, and cumin powder; dissolve with some of the beef broth and add to corned beef. Add zucchini and continue cooking until zucchini is tender, making sure it is not overcooked. This is better if allowed to stand about ½ hour before serving. Nice, served with hot tortillas. Serves 8 to 10.

BIFTEK A LA MEXICANA

(Beefsteak, Mexican Style)

1½ pounds top round steak   *½ green pepper, thinly*
    (about ½-inch thick)   *sliced*
½ cup flour   *⅓ cup oil, shortening, or*
1 teaspoon salt   *lard*
⅛ teaspoon pepper   *2 cups canned tomatoes*
1 clove garlic, minced   *(No. 303 can)*
1 large onion, thinly sliced *6 pickled waxed peppers*
                       ⅓ cup stuffed green olives

Trim excess fat from meat. Combine flour, salt, and pepper. Using the edge of a saucer, pound half the seasoned flour into one side of meat. Turn piece over and pound remaining flour into other side. Cut into individual servings, if desired. Toss into a Dutch oven or heavy skillet the garlic, onion, green pepper, and oil, or shortening, or lard. Cook until the vegetables are wilted. Remove vegetables and in remaining fat brown meat quickly to a deep brown on both sides. Lower heat, add cooked garlic, onion, and green pepper, remaining seasoned flour, and canned tomatoes. Cover and cook very slowly until meat is tender, about 1 to 1½ hours (or bake in a 350°F. oven). Now add pickled waxed peppers and stuffed green olives. If sauce has become too thick, it may be thinned slightly with a small amount of broth or tomatoes. Serves 6.

ASADO ELEGANTE DE MAMÁ

(Mama's Elegant Pot Roast)

I remember Mother adding one cup of white table wine to this pot roast, when she wanted to make it extra fancy. It looks very pretty when sliced because it shows the pieces of ham throughout the slices.

¾-pound slice uncooked ham
3 cloves garlic, mashed or
    pressed
5- or 6-pound pot roast of
    beef
   Salt and pepper
¼ cup oil
1 medium-sized onion,
    chopped

1 (No. 2½) can solid-pack
    tomatoes, chopped
1 bay leaf
¼ teaspoon thyme
1 (4 oz.) can button mush-
    rooms or a (2 oz.) jar
    pimiento-stuffed olives

Cut ham into strips 1-inch long and ½-inch wide; rub with garlic. Make pockets in meat with a sharp pointed knife and insert ham strips. Rub roast well with salt and pepper and brown on all sides in hot oil. Add onion, tomatoes, bay leaf, thyme and more salt and pepper, if needed. Cover and simmer until meat is tender, about 2 to 2½ hours. Add mushrooms or olives. Serves 8 to 10.

ALDILLA RELLENA CON CHORIZO

(Flank Steak Stuffed with Sausage)

1 large flank steak
1 clove garlic, mashed or
   pressed
½ pound chorizo
1 bunch green onions,
   chopped
¼ cup minced parsley
1 tablespoon chopped chile
   chipotle, or your
   favorite chile

1 egg, beaten
Flour
Salt
2 tablespoons oil
1 (8 oz.) can tomato sauce
½ cup broth
1 bay leaf

Place flank steak on a board and rub with garlic. Remove chorizo from casing and mix well with onions, parsley, chile, and egg. Spread this filling on steak and roll as you would a jelly roll, fastening with string or toothpicks. Dredge with flour and salt and brown on all sides in oil. Add tomato sauce, broth, and bay leaf. Cover and simmer until meat is tender. Serves 4 to 6.

ESTOFADO A LA MEXICANA

(Mexican Beef Stew)

The Irish have nothing on the Mexicans when it comes to making stew! This is so good it competes with the French ragoût.

2 pounds beef stew meat	1 teaspoon orégano, rubbed
1 large onion, minced	between palms of hands
2 cloves garlic, minced	Salt
1 green pepper, chopped	1 tablespoon chopped chile
1 cup tomato sauce	chipotle or your favorite
1 tablespoon vinegar	chile relish
	2 tablespoons flour

Place meat in heavy kettle, add onion, garlic, and green pepper; pour tomato sauce over all, then add vinegar, orégano, salt, chile chipotle, and last sprinkle the flour over all. Cook on top of stove, covered, approximately 1½ hours, or until tender. Do not use any shortening; the fat on the meat will be sufficient. Serves 6.

ESTOFADO DE RES ESTILO MAMÁ

(Mama's Beef Stew)

This is one of the easiest ways I know to make a good stew. My mother brought it from Spain when she came to Mexico.

4 tablespoons oil	3 tablespoons wine vinegar
1½ pounds lean beef stew meat	1 cup red table wine
	1 bay leaf
1 medium-sized onion, minced	½ teaspoon orégano, rubbed between palms of hands
1 clove garlic, minced	
½ cup tomato sauce	Salt and pepper

Just put everything into a big pot all at once. Cover tightly and simmer 1½ hours, or until the meat is thoroughly tender. Half an hour before the meat is ready, add carrots and potatoes— Oh, I don't know how many! How many can your family eat?

COSTILLAS DE CARNERO EMPANIZADAS
A LA ESPAÑOLA

(Breaded Lamb Chops, Spanish Style)

Never have you tasted better lamb chops—at least that's what my friends think.

1 cup fine bread crumbs	2 tablespoons oil
1 clove garlic, minced	6 lamb chops
2 tablespoons minced parsley	1 can pimientos
Salt and pepper	

Make a paste of the bread crumbs, garlic, parsley, salt, pepper, and oil. Then pound this paste into the lamb chops; fry slowly until brown and well done. Serve on hot platter with pimientos, which have been sautéed in oil. Pork chops may be used instead of lamb if you wish. Serves 6.

PIERNA DE CARNERO A LA MEXICANA

(Leg of Lamb, Mexican Style)

This leg of lamb has flavor—Mexican flavor!

2 *cloves garlic*	1 *leg of lamb, 5 to 6 pounds*
1 *tablespoon orégano*	*Salt and pepper*
1 *pinch comino (optional)*	2 *tablespoons vinegar*
1 *tablespoon chile powder*	3 *tablespoons oil*

Mash garlic, orégano, and comino into a paste; add chile powder, mix well. Make incisions in the leg of lamb with a sharp pointed knife and fill with the paste. Season. Pour vinegar and oil over meat and let stand overnight. Roast as you would any leg of lamb, uncovered, allowing 30 minutes per pound. Serves 10 to 12.

TERNERA MECHADA

(Veal Roast)

Serve this delectable veal roast with a garnish of Little Potato Pears (page 183).

¾-pound slice of ham
 5 to 6 pound veal roast
 2 tablespoons oil
  Salt and pepper

1 medium-sized onion,
  quartered
1 large leek, sliced
1 carrot, cut in large pieces
1 cup rich broth

Cut ham into strips 1-inch long and ½-inch wide. Cut slashes in veal with a sharp knife and insert pieces of ham. Rub roast with oil, salt, and pepper. Place in roasting pan and bake at 325°F. When meat starts to brown, add vegetables and baste often with the broth until all of it is used. Allow 30 minutes per pound cooking time. Strain pan gravy and pour over roast on hot platter. Serves 10 to 12.

HÍGADOS DE POLLO A LA ESPAÑOLA

(Spanish Chicken Livers)

I think these are particularly good for breakfast, when served with my Tortilla con Huevo. You might begin the meal with another Mexican specialty—sliced oranges sprinkled with cinnamon and sugar. And, of course, you'll want plenty of hot tortillas and cups and cups of coffee.

1 pound chicken livers,
   fresh or frozen
Flour
Salt and pepper
4 tablespoons butter or
   margarine, melted

1 bunch green onions,
   chopped
1 (8 oz.) can mushrooms or
   ½ pound sautéed
   mushrooms
⅓ cup sherry

Coat chicken livers with seasoned flour. Sauté in melted butter until lightly browned. Add onions and cook until tender. Pour in mushrooms (liquid and all) and sherry; simmer about 5 minutes to blend flavors. Serve on rice or toast. Serves 4.

MOLE DE OLLA

(Mole Out of a Pot)

An *olla*, as you probably know, is a big, fat-bellied clay pot, much used in Mexican kitchens. I serve this *mole* in soup plates with minced green onions sprinkled over the top and lots of hot tortillas on the side. Another thing—if it's prepared the day before and reheated, the flavor is better, just as it is with all curries and stews.

1 rack (2½ to 3 pounds)
   pork spareribs, cut in
   pieces
1½ quarts water

1 bay leaf
2 mint leaves
6 whole peppercorns
Salt

Sauce:

6 chiles pasilla
2 tablespoons sesame seeds
3 tablespoons lard

1 medium-sized onion,
   chopped
1 can tomato sauce
Salt

Cook spareribs in water with seasonings until tender. In the meantime, wash the chiles, remove seeds, and fry in lard with the sesame seeds. Drain excess lard and whirl mixture in an electric blender or grind. Wilt onion in the same lard that chiles were fried in; add tomato sauce, chile mixture, and salt. Add this sauce to spareribs and broth. Cook slowly for 15 to 20 minutes to blend flavors and take the pot right to the table. Serves 3 to 4.

CARNE MARGARITA

(Meat a la Marguerite)

This makes a very attractive platter, so I've been told, and mighty good eating, which I well know.

2 pounds cooked beef, sliced	1 tablespoon or more of your favorite green chile relish
½ pound zucchini, cooked	Oil, vinegar, and salt
1 large avocado	Shredded lettuce
2 tablespoons onion, minced	2 hard-cooked eggs
	Radishes

Mash zucchini and avocado. Add onion, chile relish, oil, vinegar, and salt. Spread avocado mixture on slice of beef. Cover with another slice to make a sandwich. Arrange meat sandwiches on platter and cover each with remaining avocado mixture. Form a marguerite on each one, using the white of egg cut in strips for the petals and little pieces of yolk for the center. Season lettuce with oil, vinegar, and salt and put all around the platter, garnished with radish rosettes.

POZOLE DE LUJO

(Luxurious Pork Stew)

This is, as the name implies, a "deluxe pozole." The ordinary way of making it is by using only pigs' head. It is a very popular dish, usually served after a *"parranda"* (a big night out).

2 pounds pigs' head, cut in
    pieces
1 pound pork loin, cut in
    pieces
1 fricassee chicken,
    disjointed
3 pigs' feet
3 quarts water

1 medium-sized onion,
    chopped
2 cloves garlic
2 or more tablespoons chile
    powder
1 pound nixtamal or 1 (No.
    2½) can hominy
Salt

Cook pigs' head, pork loin, chicken, pigs' feet, onion, and garlic in salted water for 1 hour, covered. Add nixtamal or hominy and chile powder dissolved in a little of the broth. Continue cooking until meats are tender. Serve in soup plates with hot tortillas. In center of table place small bowls containing green onions, shredded lettuce, orégano, and sliced radishes. Let each person garnish his *pozole* to taste.

LENGUA DE RES A LA VINAGRETA

(Beef Tongue a la Vinaigrette)

This is one of the dishes that I like to serve at a summer buffet. I generally serve it with many other dishes—sort of a Mexican Smörgåsbord.

1 beef tongue	1 bay leaf
1 carrot	Sprig of parsley
1 onion	Salt and pepper
2 stalks celery	

Sauce:

1 cup olive oil	1 teaspoon paprika
½ cup wine vinegar	1 teaspoon prepared
1 tablespoon chopped	mustard
parsley	3 hard-cooked eggs,
1 tablespoon chopped green	chopped
pepper	Salt and pepper
1 bunch green onions,	
chopped	

Cook tongue in boiling water with carrot, onion, celery, bay leaf, parsley, salt and pepper until tender (from 2 to 3½ hours). Allow tongue to cool in broth. Remove skin and cut in thin slices. Combine all sauce ingredients, mix well. Arrange overlapping layers of tongue on platter. Pour sauce over them and let stand in refrigerator overnight. Serve garnished with pickled pearl onions, green olives, and pickled peppers.

PUCHERO

(Spanish Boiled Dinner)

Puchero is as Spanish as were my mother and father. This is a complete meal in itself, and a favorite one when we have a family gathering. The Spanish sausage comes in cans, from Spain. If you can't find it, skip it.

1 fricassee chicken, cut in pieces	¾ pound ground pork
6 quarts water	2 eggs, beaten
Salt and pepper	½ cup grated bread crumbs
2 cups garbanzos (soak over-night in salted water)	2 tablespoons flour
6 Spanish sausages	6 potatoes, peeled and quartered
½ pound salt pork	1 bunch carrots, cut in strips
2 pounds shoulder of lamb	1 medium-sized cabbage, cut in wedges
¾ pound ground beef	

Wash chicken, cover with cold water, add salt and pepper, and boil 10 minutes, then turn down heat and let simmer for 30 minutes longer. Skim. Add drained soaked garbanzos, sausages, salt pork, and shoulder of lamb. Then add the beef and pork which have been prepared as follows: Add eggs, bread crumbs, flour, salt and pepper to beef and pork and shape into a large ball. Place this on top of the chicken et cetera, and cook until garbanzos are done, or approximately 1 hour longer. The vegetables should be added during the last 30 minutes. Serves 10 or 12.

ASADO ESTILO MAZATLÁN

(Beef, Mazatlán Style)

It is warm in Mazatlán and this dish is a favorite one which is eaten out-of-doors in the market places. Whether or not it's really hot when it is served makes little difference. It's good and it's hearty, so that's that!

2 pounds cooked beef	Shredded lettuce
¼ cup oil	1 cup #1 sauce for tostadas
2 large boiled potatoes	(page 165)
1 pound zucchini, cooked	1 sliced avocado
1 cup cooked string beans	Sliced radishes

Cut the beef in large cubes and fry in the oil until browned. Set aside and keep warm. Cut the potatoes in cubes and brown in the same oil. Season with salt and pepper. In individual dishes arrange layers of meat, hot potatoes, hot sliced zucchini, hot beans cut in small pieces, and lettuce. Divide sauce among dishes and garnish with avocado and radishes. The sauce may be used either hot or cold. Serves 4 to 6.

CARNE EN SALSA DE CHILE COLORADO

(Meat in Red Chile Sauce)

This dish is known as chile con carne in Texas. Add some beans and they call it chile con carne con frijoles. It is a famous Mexican dish that has been taken and made famous by the Lone Star State. This dish is versatile: It can be varied by adding a can of kidney beans or a can of hominy. It may also be simplified by using chile powder or Mexican red chile sauce instead of the red chiles called for here.

2 pounds beef or pork, cut in cubes	1 cup broth or bouillon
2 cups water	½ cup water in which chiles were soaked
8 chiles colorado (red chiles)	2 tablespoons flour
2 cloves garlic	2 tablespoons oil
1 teaspoon orégano	Pinch of dried cumin
	Salt

Cook meat in salted water for half an hour and save the broth. While it cooks, remove seeds and stems from chiles, parch in a heavy ungreased skillet for a couple of minutes, taking care not to burn, and soak in warm water to cover until soft; 20 minutes or longer. Grind chiles, garlic, and orégano to consistency of paste (do this in a mortar, or *molcajete,* as the Mexicans call it, in the food grinder, or, and this is the easy way, in the blender. If the latter method is used, add broth at this time). Add the broth and strain. Brown flour in oil, then gradually add the chile mixture, cumin, and salt. Combine with meat and simmer, covered, until tender, about one hour. Serves 4 to 6.

Arroz

℘ (Rice)

Next to beans and corn, the Mexicans use rice, probably because it was (and is!) so dearly loved by the Spanish. They use it in combination with other foods: peas, clams, shrimps, chicken, and the like, and it is often a base for their famous *sopa seca.*

PAELLA A LA VALENCIANA

(Paella Valencia Style)

This is a classic dish, as you all know. The typical Spanish way of preparing it is to fry the rice in oil first for a few minutes, but I have found that the flavor does not change at all doing it this way. The advantage is that everything but adding the rice can be prepared ahead of time, then, just before guests arrive, heat to boiling point, add rice and cook.

2 roasting chickens, cut in pieces

½ cup olive oil

1 rack pork spareribs, cut in small pieces

½ pound pork sausages, cut in pieces

1 large onion, chopped

2 cloves garlic, minced

1 can tomato sauce

2 teaspoons paprika

2 quarts chicken broth

1 can wet-pack shrimp, or like amount of fresh ones

1 (10 oz.) can whole baby clams

1 cup peas, fresh or frozen

12 artichoke hearts, cooked

1 can pimientos, cut in large strips

¼ cup minced parsley

3 cups uncooked rice

3 or 4 strands saffron (optional)

Salt and pepper to taste

Fry pieces of chicken in oil. Remove and brown spareribs; remove and fry sausages; remove them and to the oil in the pan add onion and wilt. Then add garlic, tomato sauce, paprika, chicken, spareribs, sausages, and broth. Use the liquid from the shrimps, too. Season and cook covered for 15 minutes. Add all other ingredients, cover again and cook over low heat for 30 minutes longer or until all liquid is absorbed. (If you are going to use saffron, brown the strands first in a dry skillet; this makes it crisp and easily broken.) When cooked, uncover and let stand for a few minutes before serving. Serve on platter, or better yet, wrap the pot in fluted yellow and red crepe paper or aluminum foil and take to the table. Serves 12.

ARROZ CON POLLO

(Rice with Chicken)

Here, again, is a classic Spanish dish that has become an important part of Mexican cuisine. If you want it extra fancy, add green pepper or canned pimiento, diced or in strips, or fresh sautéed mushrooms.

½ cup olive oil	⅛ teaspoon powdered
1 frying chicken, cut in	saffron
serving-size pieces	2½ cups chicken broth
1 small onion, chopped	Salt and pepper
1 clove garlic, minced	1 cup uncooked rice
¼ cup tomato sauce	

Heat oil, brown chicken on both sides. Add onion and garlic, fry a few minutes, then add tomato sauce, saffron dissolved in chicken broth, salt and pepper. Cover and cook for 20 minutes. Add rice, stir well, cover again and simmer for 30 minutes longer, or until all liquid has been absorbed and chicken is tender. Serves 4 to 6.

ARROZ BLANCO CON ALCACHOFAS

(White Rice with Artichokes)

How often have you wanted a casserole to serve with baked ham at a buffet? Here, I think, is the perfect accompaniment. And someone very precious to me, Grace White, food editor of *Family Circle Magazine*, seconds my opinion.

2 cups uncooked rice	12 fresh or frozen artichoke
¼ cup olive oil	hearts, cooked
1 medium-sized onion,	1 can pimientos, cut in wide
minced	strips
2 cloves garlic, minced	Salt and pepper
5 cups chicken broth	⅛ to ¼ teaspoon saffron dis-
1 cup fresh or frozen peas	solved in 1 tablespoon
	water (optional)

Fry rice in oil until lightly colored; add onion and garlic and cook 2 or 3 minutes longer. Transfer to a 2-quart casserole, add boiling broth, peas, artichokes, pimientos, salt, pepper, and saffron. Cover and bake in a 350°F. oven until all liquid has been absorbed—about 40 or 45 minutes. Serves 6 to 8.

ARROZ CON TERNERA Y JOCOQUI

(Rice with Veal and Sour Cream)

Spanish, this, and very, very good.

2 tablespoons oil	2 tablespoons minced
1½ pounds veal, cut in small	parsley
pieces	1 teaspoon paprika
1 medium-sized onion,	3 cups beef broth
chopped	1 cup uncooked rice
1 clove garlic, mashed or	1 cup sour cream
pressed	Salt and pepper to taste

Brown meat in oil. Add onion and cook a few minutes. Add garlic, parsley, paprika, and broth. Simmer, covered, for 15 minutes. Then add rice, stir, cover and cook for another 15 minutes. Slowly stir in sour cream, season to taste, cover and cook 15 minutes longer. Serves 4 to 6.

ARROZ CON JOCOQUI

(Rice and Sour Cream Casserole)

My friends think this is one of my very best dishes. Here I have simplified its making, but it tastes every bit as good. I like it for a buffet, as the main hot dish, to serve with ham, roast pork, broiled chicken, or turkey. This may also be made with macaroni or noodles or whole hominy.

¾ pound Monterey Jack   3 cups cooked rice
   cheese   Salt and pepper
3 cups sour cream, salted   ½ cup grated Cheddar
2 cans peeled green chiles,   cheese
   chopped

Cut Jack cheese in strips. Thoroughly mix sour cream and chiles. Butter a 1½ quart casserole well. Season rice with salt and pepper, if necessary. Layer rice, sour cream mixture, and cheese strips, in that order, until you finish with rice on the top. Bake in 350°F. oven for about half an hour. During the last few minutes of baking, sprinkle grated Cheddar cheese over the rice and allow it to melt before removing casserole from oven. Serves 6 to 8.

ARROZ CON "PERRITOS"

(Rice with Frankfurters)

This may not be Mexican, but my older son, Larry, is crazy about it. Because I want to please him—and I should, he's so good to me—I'm including it. *Perritos* are little dogs, and they puff up in the cooking, cute as can be.

2 tablespoons oil   ½ can tomato sauce
1 tablespoon minced onion   2½ cups water or broth
4 frankfurters, cut in   Salt and pepper
   pieces   1 cup uncooked rice

Wilt onion in oil, add frankfurters and cook a few minutes. Add tomato sauce, water or broth, salt, and pepper. Bring to boiling point, add rice, stir once, cover and simmer for 30 minutes, or until all liquid is absorbed. Serves 4.

ARROZ BLANCO

(White Rice)

This is a *sopa seca,* used a great deal in Mexico. It can be made into a casserole dish by placing alternately layers of rice and picadillo (page 88), and ending with rice dotted with butter. Place in a 350°F. oven and heat through—about 20 minutes. Another variation is to serve the rice topped with a fried egg.

¼ *cup oil*	*1 tablespoon minced*
1 cup uncooked rice	*parsley*
1 small onion, minced	*Salt and pepper*
2½ cups chicken broth, hot	

Fry rice in oil but do not brown. Remove excess oil, add onion, boiling broth, and parsley. Season, cover, and simmer for about 30 minutes or until all broth is absorbed. Serves 4 to 6.

Frijoles

❦ (Beans)

Frijoles, or beans, are as important to Mexican cuisine as tortillas. They are served at almost every meal, including breakfast, and they find their way into many appetizers, tacos, tostadas, and such. The Mexican way of cooking them is quite a project; after the beans are boiled tender they add them, a few at a time and along with some bean liquid, to some fat in a frying pan, mashing them until all are used. I have found that the method given in this chapter is just as good. I have been an American long enough to prefer the easy way!

FRIJOLES

(Basic Mexican Bean Recipe)

1 pound pink or red beans	*Salt to taste*
1½ quarts water	*½ cup lard or more*

Soak beans overnight for faster cooking. Add more water to cover and salt and cook slowly until very tender. Mash with potato masher, add very hot lard or bacon drippings (drippings improve the flavor) and continue cooking until all the fat is absorbed by the beans. Be sure to stir often to prevent sticking! Serves 6 to 8.

NOTE: If you live where pink beans are not available or do not wish to cook the beans, you may use the canned kidney beans in the following manner: Heat 4 tablespoons of fat in frying pan, mash one can of drained kidney beans, add the liquid gradually and cook until all fat has been absorbed. All beans freeze superbly.

FRIJOLES DE LA OLLA

(Boiled Beans from the Pot)

Cook beans following basic recipe, *but* do not mash or add fat. When tender, just serve in soup plates, adding rings of green onion, grated cheese, and orégano to taste. A little chile sauce may also be added, if desired.

FRIJOLES REFRITOS

(Refried Beans)

Heat additional fat in frying pan, add mashed and fried beans (see basic bean recipe, page 113), and cook, stirring until beans are completely dry. The more fat, the better, most people think.

FRIJOLES REFRITOS CON QUESO

(Refried Beans with Cheese)

Follow same procedure as for refried beans, adding cubed Monterey Jack cheese. Let cheese melt, then serve dish quickly.

FRIJOLES CHINITOS

(Crisp Mexican Refried Beans)

Re-fry fried beans until crisp!

MANERAS ATRACTIVAS DE SERVIR FRIJOLES REFRITOS

(Exciting Ways to Serve Refried Beans)

You can have lots of fun when serving refried beans. Of course, they are just wonderful as is, I think, but there are many other good things to do with them, so make a lot at one time. Remember, they can be frozen.

Vary refried beans with these special toppings:

> salted sour cream
> sour cream, salt, and chopped peeled green chiles
> strips of crisply fried tortilla

Change their taste a bit by adding:

> chicharrones
> beaten eggs (Scramble the eggs with the beans.)

In casseroles: Casseroles can be made by placing layers of fried beans alternately with crumbled chorizo (first remove the casing and fry) and pieces of Monterey or Cheddar cheese, topping with the cheese. Bake until heated through and the cheese is melted. Or, use sardines in tomato sauce in place of the chorizo. Top casseroles with squares of crisp fried tortillas.

Sandwich idea: Add thin slices of onion and tomato to refried beans for sandwich filling. (A little orégano or salsa Jalapeña may also be added if desired.)

Filling for Empanadas: Use refried beans sprinkled with grated cheese. Or add chopped green chiles and pieces of Monterey or Cheddar cheese.

Spread tostadas (totopos)—triangles of crisply fried tortillas—with refried beans, sprinkle with grated cheese, and broil until the cheese melts. Wonderful as an appetizer.

FRIJOLES PUERCOS

(Beans, Pig Style)

Don't let the name of this throw you. As you see, they contain no pork and I suppose the reason they are called pig style is that they are eaten outdoors, but not in a sty. This is a Mexican whimsey.

½ pound bacon	*½ pound Monterey Jack*
4 cups cooked Mexican	*cheese, cubed*
beans (save some of	*Chorizo, fried*
the liquid)	*1 can sardines in tomato*
	sauce

Cut bacon in small pieces; fry until crisp. Add beans, a few at a time, mashing after each addition and adding some of the bean liquid. Cook to a thick gravy, then add cheese and chorizos (be sure to remove from casing and fry first). Lastly, add the sardines cut in pieces. Heat in the *cazuela,* or casserole, in which they are to be taken to the picnic. Eat, using strips of tostadas as spoons. Serves 8.

CROQUETAS DE FRIJOL

(Bean Croquettes)

Imagine the surprise of your luncheon guests when the crispy brown croquettes turn out to be beans, flavored with chile and stuffed with cheese. They'll love them. Serve with a tossed green salad and tortillas.

2 cups cooked red or pink beans, well mashed

2 tablespoons chopped onion

½ teaspoon orégano

1 can peeled green chiles, chopped

4 tablespoons grated Parmesan cheese

Salt to taste

¼ pound Monterey Jack or Cheddar cheese

1 egg, beaten with 1 tablespoon water

Bread crumbs

Oil for frying

Combine mashed beans, onion, orégano, chopped chiles, Parmesan cheese, and salt. Mix thoroughly and make into croquettes, placing a small piece of Monterey or Cheddar cheese in the center of each. Be sure that the cheese is well covered with the bean mixture. Roll in crumbs, then beaten egg, then crumbs again and fry in deep fat or oil until brown. Makes 6 to 8 croquettes. Serve with chile sauce.

HABAS A LA ESPAÑOLA

(Horse Beans, Spanish Style)

The Mexicans, like the Spanish, use *habas,* or horse beans, also called *fève* by the French, *fava* by the Italians. If you can't find them, use lima beans in these recipes.

⅓ cup butter or margarine
1 small onion, minced
½ cup flour
⅛ teaspoon nutmeg
    Salt and pepper to taste
2½ cups chicken or beef
    broth
3 egg yolks, slightly beaten

2 tablespoons lemon juice,
    strained
¼ cup finely-chopped
    parsley
2 pimientos, chopped
4 cups hot cooked horse
    beans or lima beans

Wilt onion in ¼ of the butter. Blend in flour, nutmeg, salt, and pepper. Stir in broth, slowly. Cook until mixture is thickened and smooth, stirring frequently, about 10 to 15 minutes. Turn heat very low and beat in egg yolks, remaining butter, and lemon juice. Cook 2 or 3 minutes longer. Remove from heat and stir briskly; then add parsley, pimientos, and beans.

NOTE: Sauce may be well covered and stored in refrigerator for several days, if desired. When ready to serve, combine sauce with beans and heat in oven before serving. Makes about 1 pint sauce. Serves 8.

HABAS ENVINADAS ESTILO MAMÁ

(Horse Beans with Wine, Mother's Way)

This was one of my father's favorites.

4 tablespoons olive oil
1 onion, minced
1 clove garlic, minced
¾ cup cubed smoked ham
2 tablespoons minced
    parsley

2 cups fresh horse or lima
    beans, shelled and
    washed
1 cup white table wine
Salt and pepper to taste

Wilt onion in oil, add garlic, ham, and parsley and cook for a few minutes; add beans, wine, salt, and pepper. Cover very tightly and simmer for about 40 minutes or until beans are tender. Serves 4.

GARBANZOS EN TOMATE

(Chick Peas in Tomato Sauce)

Mexicans and Spaniards like garbanzos and so do I. If you wish, you may substitute the cooked canned kind for the dried ones in this recipe.

1 pound garbanzos, soaked
    overnight
1½ quarts water
2 cloves garlic
1 medium-sized onion,
    chopped

⅓ cup olive oil
2 cups solid-pack canned
    tomatoes
1 can pimientos, cut in large
    strips
Salt and pepper to taste

Drain garbanzos and add the water, garlic, onion, and olive oil. Cook for an hour, then add the tomatoes and continue cooking until the garbanzos are tender. During the last 10 minutes of cooking add the pimientos. Serves 4.

POTAGE DE GARBANZO

(Chick Pea Pottage)

The seed for Mexican garbanzos comes from Spain, as do the seeds of the pimientos. They have to be replaced every few years because the soil of Mexico does funny things to them. The garbanzos get tough and the pimientos hot!

½ cup olive oil
1 medium-sized onion,
   chopped
3 cloves garlic, minced

1 pound garbanzos, soaked
   overnight
1½ quarts water
Salt and pepper to taste

Wilt onion and garlic in oil, add garbanzos, water, salt, and pepper. Cook slowly until very, very tender. This is usually served preceding the entree, as you would an Italian paste. Serves 6 to 8.

LENTEJAS CON FRUTA

(Lentils with Fruit)

Lentils with bananas or pineapple? OK, let's not have any remarks until you try it. My sister, Maria Escalambre, says that when she wants a special favor from her husband, she serves him this. Such are the wiles of women.

3 slices bacon, cut in small   2 quarts water
    pieces   ½ cup tomato sauce
1 medium-sized onion,   Salt and pepper to taste
    chopped   Sliced bananas or pine-
1 pound lentils   apple cubes

Fry bacon and onion, add rest of ingredients, except fruit. Cook slowly, until lentils are tender and liquid is thick, about 1½ hours. Serve with sliced bananas or cubes of pineapple. Serves 6 to 8.

CHILE BEANS FOR THE CROWD

I don't know many Texans, but I'd like to. One that I'd especially like to meet is Julie Benell, Food Editor of the Dallas *Morning News,* because she has shown such interest in my other books. For them, as well as others, here is a recipe for cooking beans in Texas style, rather than in the typical Mexican way. This recipe is popular and an easy way to feed a large party. It's very good with barbecued meats. This makes enough for 25 servings.

3 pounds Mexican pink   6 medium-sized onions,
    beans or kidney beans   chopped
Water   6 cloves garlic, chopped
Salt (about 2 table-   Pepper to taste
    spoons)   3 (8 oz.) cans tomato sauce
4½ pounds ground beef   3 tablespoons chile powder
    chuck   (or more if desired)
1 cup oil   —And a very large kettle!

Wash and inspect beans; cover with cold water and let soak for several hours or overnight. Put to cook in the same water in which beans were soaked; cover, and let simmer slowly. After beans have cooked for about an hour, add salt to taste (2 teaspoons for each pound of beans is the general rule). Meanwhile, in a big skillet heat the oil and in it lightly brown the meat with the chopped onions and garlic, adding salt and pepper to taste, and stirring frequently; add to the partially cooked beans, together with the tomato sauce and chile powder. Continue cooking, covered, until beans are very tender—4 to 5 hours in all for this quantity of beans. During the last hour or so of cooking, remove cover so that beans will cook down to a rich consistency. If the recipe is divided into thirds, cooking time will be shortened to about 2½ to 3 hours.

Masa

🍃 (Corn)

The use of *masa* is one of the most important features of Mexican cookery. Made from corn, in the same way that it was done centuries ago before the advent of the Spanish conquerors, the old process of making *masa* by hand was a laborious one. First the *nixtamal* had to be made. That is dried corn which is cooked in a lime solution until the husks can be rubbed off. It is then ground, while still moist, to make *masa*. The old way was to use a stone *metate*—a sort of sloping oblong stone that stands on little legs—and a stone rolling pin, or *metlalpil* (also *metclapil*). This job took muscles and patience. Today, modern machinery has taken over and except for remote spots in the country the Mexican housewife buys her *masa* ready prepared. This she uses for making tortillas, tamales, and other special Mexican dishes. Americans who live where there is a Mexican population can usually buy fresh *masa,* or if not that, they can almost certainly get *masa* flour, which is dried *masa* that needs only to be mixed with water. Even in parts of the United States far from Mexican influence, grocers should be able to order this flour for you, as it is made by a large American company.

If that is too difficult, write to one of the stores listed on pages 4–5; they will send it to you.

Tortillas, except for the flour tortilla (page 126), are made from *masa*. The old, and still the best, way was to make them by hand. A ball of moist *masa,* about the size of an egg, is patted rhythmically between the palms of the hands until a flat round cake is formed. It is a fascinating thing to watch; the Mexicans do it so casually that it looks very easy. "Looks easy," I say, but my American friends who have tried it think otherwise. After the tortilla is formed, it is cooked on a griddle, preferably one made of soapstone, until it is done on both sides. It is not browned. Today, even in Mexico, few women make their own tortillas, though some still do, using a press to form them. Many buy machine-made tortillas which are also available in stores handling fancy groceries throughout most of the country. If you can't get them, get some tortilla flour and follow directions on the package. Tortillas may be pressed by putting a ball of *masa* between two sheets of Saran or other plastic, and pressing flat with a bread board. If, after cooking, tortillas dry out, I simply dampen my hand and rub it over the surface of the tortilla. This makes it just moist enough to freshen it before reheating. And that reminds me, tortillas should be served hot. I heat them directly on a low gas flame, turning them almost constantly as they heat. They may also be done on an electric burner, or on a hot griddle. The Mexican way is to put them in a hot dish and cover them with a napkin to keep them hot until serving time.

NOTE ON TORTILLAS

In Oaxaca, a special dish called *flanta,* or flute, is made with masa. Actually it is a large corn tortilla that is made by spreading a ball of masa on the griddle by hand, then scraping off the surplus dough. It is about 12 inches in diameter and is rolled like a flute, and filled with beans, meat and chile.

TACOS

Tacos, considered the Mexican sandwich, have become tremendously popular in the West and Southwest. Tacos are tortillas that are rolled or folded (page 128) and stuffed with various fillings. They may be just warmed tortillas, filled, rolled, and eaten without further ado, or they may be grilled, fried, or baked. I prefer the baked ones, as they may be prepared ahead of time and put in the oven to heat just before serving. They are especially good served with a green tossed salad and refried beans. When making tacos, the tortillas should be fresh. If not, they should be heated to soften them and prevent them from cracking when they are rolled.

Tacos may be served plain or with any desired sauce over them.

NOTE ON MEXICAN BREADS

Don't think for a minute that tortillas are the *only* bread of Mexico. Actually, Mexican rolls and bread made from wheat flour have that marvelous flavor characteristic of European breads—nutty and delicious. The rolls are made in many different shapes, and each one bears a different whimsical name. The *bolillo,* or shuttle shape, is the most common, but there are others. The *pambazo,* for instance, is a crusty roll, hollow in the middle. It is sometimes split, filled with an enchilada and shredded lettuce (for feathers!) and called a *guajolote,* or turkey! Then there are many sweet rolls. These when shell-shaped are called *conchas;* when book-shaped, *libros;* when fat and wiggly, *gusanos* (worms); and on and on. The dough from which these *pan dulce* are made is called the *alma,* or soul, and indeed it seems alive, for it is made from yeast.

Totopos mean different things to different people. To some they are small round tortillas, about the size of a silver dollar, fried crisp so that they curl slightly. To others they are wedges of tortilla,

fried in deep fat. These I usually call *tostaditas*. Still others call
small garnished *tostadas, totopos,* and I have even known a tortilla,
spread with chile sauce and folded, to be called by this name.

Quesadillas are sometimes filled with finely-chopped squash
flowers mixed with a little peeled green chile, and with plenty of
grated cheese.

Though *quesadillas* originally were always filled with cheese, they
are now sometimes filled with meat, poultry, or fish.

ENCHILADAS

Enchiladas are tortillas that are dipped in sauce, then fried lightly,
filled with various fillings, and rolled. Sometimes the tortillas are
fried before dipping in the sauce. I like the first way because I think
the flavor is better, but I admit it takes more skill to do it this way
unless you don't mind making a mess.

TORTILLAS DE HARINA
(Flour Tortillas)

Tortillas, the bread of Mexico, are usually made of nixtamal,
or lye-treated corn (page 123), but in some parts of Mexico, especially Sonora, flour tortillas are popular. They are easy to make at
home.

4 cups flour	*½ cup shortening*
2 teaspoons salt	*1 cup lukewarm water*

Sift flour and salt into mixing bowl. Add shortening and mix until well distributed. Add lukewarm water and blend well. Turn out
on lightly-floured board and knead about 50 strokes. Divide dough
into 12 equal-sized pieces and form each piece into a ball. Cover

with a cloth and let stand for 15 minutes. Roll each ball into a round tortilla, 8 inches in diameter. Cook on a moderately hot ungreased skillet until golden brown in spots, turning once and being careful not to break air bubbles. Makes 12 tortillas.

In certain parts of Mexico huge flour tortillas are made, some two feet in diameter. It is fascinating to watch them being made! They are patted and patted out until they extend halfway up the worker's arm, then are pulled and patted even thinner, before cooking on the griddle. Reheated in a hot oven until crisp, then brushed with melted butter, they are delicious.

Burritos, known only in northern Mexico and across the border are flour tortillas, filled with fried beans, or beans and meat, then rolled, with the sides tucked in like a blanket-roll on a camping trip.

TOSTADAS

(Crisp Fried Tortillas)

Tostadas are, as the name implies, tortillas that have been fried crisp. They may be bought at Mexican stores already fried, or made at home by frying tortillas in oil until golden brown and crisp. As a time-saving hint, they may be fried the day before and crisped in the oven just before using. Originally *tostadas* were made from *raspadas,* hand-made tortillas with the "face" or top layer peeled off before frying. They are covered with many combinations and different sauces and garnishes. A meal in themselves, they usually combine with an entree and salad, and are delightful for a festive luncheon or supper.

NOTE: All ingredients for *tostadas* may be prepared ahead of time but they should never be assembled until ready to serve because they would get soggy.

Tostadas are very flexible. If they are served as an entree, they should be made with more filling than when served for luncheon or snacks. If they do not contain beans, they are delicious served with refried beans.

When I speak of *tostaditas* in this book, I mean tortillas cut in sections and fried crisp. These are also called *totopos,* and I explain them elsewhere.

TACOS DE CARNE MOLIDA

(Ground Beef Tacos)

Another way to make these is to soften the tortilla in about an inch of oil in a skillet, then fold it and continue frying until crisp, holding them together with a pair of tongs or pressing down lightly with a spatula. They are then filled with the hot meat filling, the lettuce is tucked in at the top, along with the garnish, a little taco sauce is drizzled over all, and they are eaten at once, in the hand, like a sandwich. This method may be more American than Mexican, but so what?

12 tortillas

Oil for frying

Filling:

2 tablespoons oil
1 large onion, chopped
1 pound lean ground beef
1 small green pepper, chopped
2 medium-sized tomatoes, peeled and chopped or one cup solid-pack tomatoes
1 clove garlic, mashed or pressed

1 or more tablespoons green chile relish
1 teaspoon orégano, rubbed between palms of hands
1 teaspoon vinegar
Salt
¼ cup blanched, slivered almonds (optional)
Shredded lettuce, avocado wedges, pickled baby beets

Fry meat and onion in oil until brown; add green pepper, tomatoes, garlic, chile relish, orégano, vinegar, and salt. Cook for 15 minutes. Add almonds, if you are using them. Warm tortillas to soften, spread some of the meat filling in each, roll and fry, seam side down, to desired crispness. Serve with lettuce to which you may add oil, vinegar, and salt, if you wish. Garnish with the avocado and beets. Serves 6 to 12.

ENCHILADAS VERDES

(Green Enchiladas)

12 tortillas   *Oil for frying*

Sauce:

1 can peeled green chiles   *¼ cup oil*
1 medium-sized green   *Salsa Jalapeña, or your*
  pepper   *favorite green chile rel-*
3 (10 oz.) cans tomatillo   *ish, to taste*
1 medium-sized onion,   *Salt*
  peeled   *½ cup finely chopped*
2 cloves garlic, peeled   *parsley*
1 large tomato, peeled, or
  ¾ cup solid-pack
  canned tomatoes

Filling:

2 pounds lean boneless pork,   *1 large tomato, peeled and*
  cut in small pieces   *chopped or ¾ cup solid-*
2 cloves garlic, peeled   *pack tomatoes*
¼ cup water   *3 tablespoons grated*
Salt   *Parmesan or Romano*
1 medium-sized onion,   *cheese*
  chopped

Remove seeds from green chiles and green pepper and cut in strips. Drain one can of tomatillo, but use the other two cans undrained. Place chiles, pepper, tomatillo, onion, garlic, and tomato in electric blender, using about ⅓ of these ingredients at a time. Blend but not too much. If blender is not available, put through fine blade of food grinder. Heat oil, add blended mixture and salt, and simmer for about 5 or 10 minutes. Add salsa Jalapeña and simmer a few minutes longer. Add parsley.

Make the filling by putting pork, garlic, water, and salt in a skillet. Cover and simmer for half an hour. Uncover and cook until meat starts to brown, stirring occasionally. Add onion and tomato and simmer until almost all liquid is absorbed—about 15 or 20 minutes. Now dip tortillas, one at a time, into green sauce, fry lightly in oil, add filling, roll and place in a shallow glass baking dish and pour remaining sauce over them. Sprinkle generously with grated cheese. Keep warm until serving.

These enchiladas are always made with pork, but if you do not like pork, they could be made with cooked, cubed chicken, moistened with a little of the sauce.

SOPES DE SARDINAS

(Sardine Masa Patties)

Tricky, these, but amusing and good. If you find it too hard to make oblong sopes they may be round. They can also be filled with tuna, chicken, chopped chorizo, meats, or what-have-you.

Sopes:

2 cups fresh masa
3 tablespoons shortening
1 tablespoon chile powder, dissolved in 2 tablespoons water or broth

3 tablespoons grated
    Parmesan cheese
Salt
Oil for frying

Filling:

1 tablespoon oil
1 small onion, chopped
1 large tomato, peeled and
    chopped
1 cup fried beans (page 113)

1 can sardines in oil, boned
    and shredded
Lettuce and radishes
Parmesan cheese, grated
Your favorite chile relish

Mix masa, shortening, chile powder, cheese, and salt until smooth. Divide into 12 even balls. Pat each ball between palms of hands into an oblong shape, 3-inches long by 2-inches wide. Pinch up edges between thumb and fingers to form a little border. This is a *sope.* Fry on both sides in hot oil until brown. Place on absorbent paper and keep warm.

For filling, wilt onion in hot oil, add tomato and beans, fry until almost dry; then add sardines. Fill each sope with this filling, add a little of your favorite chile sauce on top, sprinkle with cheese and garnish with lettuce and radishes.

TAMAL DE CAZUELA CON POLLO

(Tamale Casserole with Chicken)

This is an authentic tamale pie, made with fresh masa. You can buy it at Mexican markets. It will be worth all the trouble you have to go to to find it, I promise.

3 large eggs, separated
½ pound fresh masa
1 cup whipping cream

¼ cup soft butter or
    margarine
Salt
1 teaspoon baking powder

Filling:

2 tablespoons oil or butter
1 small onion, chopped
3 large tomatoes, peeled and
    chopped or 2 cups solid-
    pack canned tomatoes
1 can peeled green chiles,
    chopped

2 cups cooked, cubed
    chicken
1 small jar stuffed olives,
    drained
½ cup raisins plumped in hot
    water and drained
Salt
Grated Parmesan cheese

Beat egg whites until stiff and set aside. Blend masa and cream thoroughly, add butter or margarine and beat well. Stir in salt. Add egg yolks, one at a time, beating well after each addition. Add baking powder and fold in egg whites.

For the filling: Wilt onion in hot oil or butter, add tomatoes. Cook a few minutes, then add chiles, chicken, olives, raisins, and salt. Cook a few minutes more.

Place half of the masa mixture at the bottom of a 2-quart casserole, top with filling, and cover with remaining masa. Bake 45 minutes in a 350°F. oven. Sprinkle with cheese and bake 15 minutes longer. Serves 6.

NOTE: If gravy is too thin, it may be thickened with a little flour or cornstarch.

TORTA DE PUERCO CON TOMATILLO

(Pork and Tomatillo Casserole)

The tomatillo gives this an entirely different flavor—a taste for which, they say, has to be acquired. I wouldn't know because I've always liked it.

10 tortillas, or flour tortillas (page 126)

Oil for frying

Sauce:

1 tablespoon oil
1 medium-sized onion, chopped
2 (10 oz.) cans tomatillo, puréed
2 cloves garlic, mashed or pressed
Salt
1 pint sour cream, salted

1 can peeled green chiles, chopped
1 cup chopped, cooked pork
1 cup sliced, cooked zucchini
1 small jar stuffed green olives

Fry tortillas lightly in oil and drain on absorbent paper. For the sauce, wilt onion in oil, add tomatillo, garlic, and salt. Cook for 15 to 20 minutes. Set aside. Mix sour cream and chiles. Set aside. Butter a 2-quart casserole and arrange alternate layers of tortillas, pork, zucchini, the sour cream mixture and olives, until all ingredients have been used, ending with a layer of sour cream. Bake at 325°F. for about 30 to 40 minutes. To serve, cut as you would cake. You'll want refried beans with this, if our tastes agree. Serves 6.

TORTA DE GALLINA CON CHIPOTLE

(Chicken and Chipotle Casserole)

I think this is exceptionally good because it can be prepared ahead of time. My guests always like it.

10 tortillas, or flour tortillas   *Oil for frying*
    (page 126)

Filling:

1 cup chopped cooked   *2 tablespoons chopped ripe*
    chicken   *olives*
2 tablespoons blanched,   *3 cups chile chipotle sauce*
    chopped almonds   *(page 168)*
2 tablespoons chopped   *¾ cup cubed Monterey Jack*
    seedless raisins   *cheese*

Fry tortillas lightly in oil and drain on absorbent paper. Combine chicken, almonds, raisins, and olives and mix well. Set aside. Butter a 2-quart casserole and place a tortilla in it, then a layer of filling, one of sauce and cheese and another tortilla. Repeat until all tortillas and filling have been used; pour remaining sauce over all; top with remaining cheese and bake at 350°F. for about 30 minutes. To serve, cut as you would a cake. Serves 6.

TACOS DE PAPA Y CHORIZO

(Chorizo and Potato Tacos)

They do these often in Mexico. The people, as a whole, are not wealthy, so they have learned to make a little meat go a long way. They stretch its flavor with beans, potatoes, and tortillas.

12 tortillas   *Oil for frying*

Filling:

3 chorizos (½ pound)   *Salt*
2 cups cooked, cubed   *1 cup tomatillo sauce (page*
    potatoes   *166) or your favorite*
1 or more tablespoons chile   *taco sauce*
    chipotle, chopped   *½ pint sour cream, salted*

Remove chorizos from casing and fry without fat. When they are well done, add potatoes, chile, and salt. Mix well. Warm tortillas to soften them; place some of the filling on each one; roll and fry seam side down to desired crispness. Arrange on hot platter and to each taco, add a little tomatillo sauce and a spoonful of sour cream. Serve at once to 6 or 12.

TACOS DE GALLINA

(Chicken Tacos)

12 tortillas   *Oil for frying*

Filling:

*2 tablespoons butter or
    margarine*

*1 medium-sized onion,
    chopped*

*2 medium-sized tomatoes,
    peeled and chopped or
    1 cup solid-pack to-
    matoes*

*4 pickled wax peppers,
    chopped*

*2 cups cooked, cubed
    chicken*

Salt

*Shredded lettuce, avocado,
    and stuffed green olives*

Wilt onion in butter, add tomatoes, cook a few minutes and add peppers, chicken, and salt. Warm tortillas to soften them; put some of the filling in each; roll and fry, seam down to desired crispness. Serve with lettuce to which a little oil, vinegar, and salt may be added. Garnish with wedges of avocado and slices of olives. Serves 6 or 12.

TACOS VERDE, BLANCO Y COLORADO

(Green, White and Red Tacos)

Red, white, and green—what a color scheme for a dish of wonderful chicken-filled tacos!

12 tortillas   Oil for frying

Sauce:

1 tablespoon oil   1 or more tablespoons
1 small onion, chopped   chopped chile chipotle or
1 can tomato sauce or   your favorite chile relish
    purée   Salt

Filling:

2 cups cooked, cubed   ½ pint sour cream, salted
    chicken (preferably   1 cup guacamole (page 8)
    white meat)   Pickled pearl onions or
¼ cup grated Parmesan   onion rings
    cheese

For sauce, wilt onion in oil; add tomato sauce, chile, and salt. Cook until sauce is thick.

Fry tortillas lightly in oil, and on each put some chicken and some cheese; roll and arrange on hot platter. Over the top spread one wide strip of guacamole, one of sour cream and one of sauce. This gives the effect of green, white, and red of the Mexican flag. Garnish with pickled onions, or onion rings. Serves 6 or 12.

TACOS DE SESOS

(Lamb Brain Tacos)

I hope you are not prejudiced against eating brains, as these tacos are extra good. Mexicans, like the French, consider brains epicurean fare.

6 tortillas	1 tablespoon minced onion
1½ pounds brains	1 large tomato, peeled and
1 clove garlic	chopped
1 bay leaf	2 peeled green chiles,
Sprig of parsley	chopped
1 tablespoon vinegar	Salt
2 tablespoons butter or	Shredded lettuce
margarine	Radishes

Remove membranes from brains and soak in cold water for 20 minutes. Drain and cook in 1 quart of water with garlic, bay leaf, parsley, vinegar, and salt, for 20 minutes. Drain, pat dry, and cut in small cubes. Wilt onion in butter; add tomato; fry a few minutes, then add brains and chiles. Cook until almost dry. Warm tortillas to soften them; fill with brain mixture and fry to desired crispness. Serve with shredded lettuce and garnish with radish slices. Serves 6.

TACOS DE GALLINA CON SALSA DE CHIPOTLE

(Chicken Tacos with Chipotle Sauce)

You'd almost think this recipe was developed at California Foods Research Institute, it's so chockful of the products they so ably promote. You will find that these tacos, even though fried, cut easily with a fork, so they can be served more formally than most.

8 tortillas   *Oil for frying*

2 eggs, beaten

Filling:

1 cup coarsely chopped, cooked chicken

1 tablespoon chopped seedless raisins

1 tablespoon blanched and chopped almonds

1 tablespoon chopped ripe olives

2 cups chile chipotle sauce (page 168)

Avocado

Lettuce

Combine all the filling ingredients together and mix well. Set aside. Dip tortillas, one at a time, in egg; spread some of the filling on each; roll and fry, seam down, in hot oil to desired crispness. Arrange on platter, pour heated chipotle sauce over tacos. Garnish with wedges of avocado and lettuce. Serve at once to 4 or 8.

TACOS CON SALSA DE TOMATILLO

(Tacos with Tomatillo Sauce)

8 tortillas   *Oil for frying*

Sauce:

2 tablespoons oil

2 cans tomatillo, put through blender or sieved

2 cloves garlic, mashed or pressed

1 can peeled green chiles, chopped

Salt

Filling:

1 small package cream cheese
3 tablespoons thin cream
1 cup chopped, cooked pork
   or chicken

Salt
Onion rings
Radishes, sliced thin

For sauce, heat oil, add tomatillo, garlic, chiles, and salt. Cook for 10 to 15 minutes. Set aside. For filling, cream the cheese with the cream; add pork or chicken and salt; set aside. Dip tortillas in the sauce, one at a time; remove and fry lightly in oil. Put some filling on each tortilla, roll and arrange on a shallow glass baking dish or on a platter. Pour remaining sauce over tacos, garnish with onions and radishes and serve at once. These tacos are extra good served with 1 tablespoon of salted sour cream on top. Serves 4 to 8.

NOTE: If you like them more spicy, add more peeled green chiles or chile relish to the sauce.

TACOS DE JOCOQUI AL HORNO
(Baked Sour Cream Tacos)

12 tortillas

Oil for frying

Sauce:

2 tablespoons oil
1 small onion, chopped
1 (No. 2½) can solid-pack
   tomatoes, chopped
1 teaspoon orégano, rubbed
   between palms of hands

2 or more tablespoons salsa
   Jalapeña, or your favorite chile relish
Salt
1 pound Monterey Jack
   cheese, cubed
1 pint sour cream, salted

For sauce, wilt onion in hot oil. Add tomatoes, orégano, salsa Jalapeña, and salt. Cook for 15 to 20 minutes. Set aside. Fry tortillas lightly in oil, put some of the sauce and a piece of cheese on each one and roll. Arrange in a buttered shallow glass baking dish. Pour remaining sauce over tacos, top with cheese and spoon sour cream over all. Bake at 325°F. for 25 to 30 minutes. Serves 6 to 12.

TACOS DE JOCOQUI Y CHILE VERDE

(Sour Cream and Green Chile Tacos)

You know who likes this dish as well as I? Genevieve Callahan, that's who. She includes a recipe for Tacos de Crema in *The New California Cook Book*. Her version is a little different than this, but who could resist either result?

12 tortillas
  Oil for frying
1 tablespoon butter or
  margarine
1 tablespoon minced onion
1 cup half milk and half
  cream

1 pint sour cream
1 can peeled green chiles,
  chopped
1 pound Monterey Jack
  cheese, cut into 12 strips
Salt

Wilt onion in butter, add light cream and salt. Set aside. Mix sour cream with chiles and salt. Set aside. Fry tortillas lightly in hot oil, dip into light cream mixture, one at a time. Put a strip of cheese on each, roll and arrange on a buttered shallow baking dish. Pour remaining light cream mixture over tacos and spoon sour cream mixture over them. Bake at 325°F. for 25 to 30 minutes. Serves 6 or 12.

For variation, these tacos may be filled with refried beans, with or without the cheese.

TAMALES

Tamales are unknown in Spain, but they have been made in Mexico for centuries. The name itself comes from the Aztec word, *tamalli.* Unlike other Mexican dishes made with masa, tamales are pretty much the same all over Mexico, being corn husks spread with masa and wrapped around savory fillings. There are variations in the wrappings, however. In Mexico, for instance, they are usually folded over and tied at one end only, while in the United States they are usually larger and sausage-like in shape, with more sauce or gravy in the filling, and they are tied at both ends. Also, in some parts of Mexico—Oaxaca, for instance—banana leaves are used in place of dried corn husks. Sometimes green corn husks are used to wrap fresh corn tamales, and often tamale fillings are sweet. These are usually served on special occasions, often at a party called a *tamalada.*

TAMALES (BASIC RECIPE)

1½ pounds dried corn husks (approximately)
1½ pounds shortening (preferably lard)
5 pounds masa (page 123)
1 cup chicken, pork or beef broth
5 teaspoons baking powder
1 tablespoon salt

Remove silk from husks and soak in warm water for at least an hour. Beat shortening to the consistency of whipping cream, mix with masa, broth, baking powder, and salt, and continue beating until the mixture is so fluffy that a spoonful of it, dropped into a cup of cold water will rise to the top. Drain soaked husks, shaking off the excess water, and proceed in one of the following ways:

TAMALES MEXICAN STYLE

Select a wide husk or two narrower ones, and spread husk with about 2 tablespoons of prepared masa, having it come clear to the sides and about an inch or two from the bottom, but only half way up toward the pointed end. Now put on a spoonful of the desired filling and fold sides of husk together, completely covering it. (If two husks are used, use only one tablespoon masa on the second one, put the second one over the seam of the first one, having it point in the opposite direction—pointed part toward the bottom.) Now fold the tamale in half and tie at the top with a strip of corn husk. Clip off surplus husk and ends of tie with scissors. You now have a little corn husk bag, filled with masa and filling, and tied at the top. Steam for 45 minutes. These freeze beautifully and can be reheated by steaming in the frozen state for 30 to 45 minutes, depending on size.

TAMALES AMERICAN STYLE

Spread the husks as for the Mexican tamales, but use at least two and sometimes three or four husks, so that the more moist filling will be well sealed in. Spread the first husk—a wide one—with 2 tablespoons of masa, and add more filling than for the other kind. Add other husks, each one spread with 1 tablespoon of masa, taking care that each one completely covers the seam of the previous one, and that each husk points in the opposite direction from the one that precedes it. Twist tamale tight at both ends and tie with strips of corn husk or string. These should be steamed over hot water for an hour; they also freeze.

NOTE: The amount of masa in the above recipe is sufficient for 3 dozen medium-sized tamales.

SALSA PARA TAMALES

(Tamale Sauce)

1 cup oil
1 cup flour
3 (8 oz.) cans tomato sauce
2 (10 oz.) cans red chile sauce
   (available at Mexican
   stores)

Salt
Ripe olives, pitted
   preferred

Brown the flour slightly in hot oil, add tomato sauce, chile sauce, and salt. Cook for a few minutes or until thickened. Add meat, prepared as in Meat for Tamales (page 145). Allow sauce to cool completely before using for tamales because it's easier to handle. Add one ripe olive per tamale along with filling. The above amount will yield about 1½ quarts of sauce.

NOTE: Mexicans do not use a great deal of sauce in tamales. However, I find that Americans like more and more and more sauce, so you may have to double the above recipe.

I am not giving the old-fashioned way of making tamale sauce, because it requires a lot of time and work. I find that there are many very good prepared chile sauces on the market that contain all the spices and chile needed. My personal preference is to combine the red chile sauce with tomato; however, if you prefer, you may use the red chile sauce without tomato, diluted with water or broth to suit your "peppery" taste.

CARNE PARA TAMALES

(Meat for Tamales)

5 pounds lean pork or beef,   *3 cloves garlic, peeled*
    cut in large cubes   *Salt*
1 cup water

Cook meat with water, garlic, and salt until tender. Remove garlic, drain meat and add to tamale sauce. Cooked chicken, either boned or boneless, may also be used in place of pork or beef, and so can any leftover cooked meat or poultry.

OTROS RELLENOS PARA TAMALES

(Other Tamale Fillings)

Pork with green chile sauce (page 169) with pickled wax peppers, or pickled vegetables and green olives added. Pieces of cooked, cubed chicken may be used instead of the pork in this recipe.

Picadillo (page 88).

Pieces of Monterey Jack cheese wrapped with strips of peeled green chiles. These tamales are usually made smaller.

Beans with cheese and strips of peeled green chiles.

On the west coast of Mexico tamales are made with stewed chicken, fresh tomato, or your favorite tomato sauce, pickled string beans, pickled onions, pickled wax peppers, and stuffed green olives. These are made with just enough sauce to moisten the chicken.

TAMALITOS DE COCTEL

(Cocktail Tamales)

I suppose I am crazy to give my recipe for *tamalitos,* for selling them, as well as *tacos, tortillas* and such, is the way my sons and I make our living. Still, you may realize how little we charge after you've made a batch yourself, so maybe I'm not so dumb after all.

Serve these with tea, or *merienda,* or with cocktails. I have them steaming hot and snip off an end with scissors. Guests eat them by drawing them through the teeth so that they get the filling but not the husks. If they are extra large, like my commercial ones, they may be cut in half. Each half is a good bite.

¾ pound shortening	*1 teaspoon salt*
2½ pounds masa	*2 teaspoons baking powder*
½ cup broth	

Beat lard to the consistency of whipped cream, gradually add masa alternately with chicken broth. Add salt and baking powder and continue beating until mixture is so fluffy that when a little of it is dropped in a cup of cold water it will float to the top.

Tamalitos: Separate ½ pound of corn husks, remove the silks and soak in warm water for about ten minutes. Wash thoroughly and drain. Place one teaspoon of the masa mixture in each husk, spread and add desired filling. Roll and turn the long ends up, tie with a strip of the husk—or they may be tied at both ends, and steam for 30 minutes. This yields about 6 dozen tamalitos.

Fillings: Chopped, cooked ham with coarsely grated Cheddar cheese and a little Tabasco sauce to taste. Stuffed green olives, cut in half. Deviled ham also zipped up with Tabasco sauce. Anchovies. Monterey Jack cheese wrapped with strips of green chile. And as many other fillings as you can think of. Tamalitos freeze well and just need steaming over boiling water for 20 minutes before serving. The same fillings that are used for the large tamales may be used in these, but the meat should be chopped smaller.

TAMALITOS DE DULCE

(Sweet Tamales)

I always think of Marian Manners of the Los Angeles *Times* when I make tamales because she is so very fond of them. And I am very fond of her—she has been a true friend through the years.

½ *pound lard, or* ¼ *pound butter and* ¼ *cup lard*	1 *teaspoon salt*
1½ *pounds fresh masa*	1 *teaspoon cinnamon or anise*
¼ *cup chicken broth*	1 *teaspoon baking powder*
1 *cup sugar*	

Beat lard to the consistency of whipped cream. Gradually add masa alternately with broth. Add salt, sugar, cinnamon, and baking powder and continue beating until the mixture is so fluffy that when a little of it is dropped in a cup of cold water it will float to the top. This amount of masa is enough for about 50 to 55 tamalitos.

Making tamalitos: Separate ½ pound dry corn husks, remove silks, and soak husks in warm water for about 10 minutes; then wash thoroughly and drain. Place 1 teaspoon of masa in each husk and spread. This will make a bite-size tamalito. Put desired filling in the center, roll and turn up the long end, tie with a strip of the husk and steam for 30 minutes.

The following fillings may be used: apricot or strawberry preserves; coconut; well-drained fruit cocktail; blanched almonds or pine nuts and raisins; citron and pine nuts; candied cherries; candied pineapple; pressed quince. Food coloring may be added to the masa for variations. These freeze and keep indefinitely.

QUESADILLA

(Tortilla with Filling)

Here's a snack for a husky man though I have seen a dainty little woman make short work of them, too. They are quick and easy.

Take fresh tortillas, place a generous piece of Monterey, Cheddar, or American cheese, a teaspoon of salsa Jalapeña, a piece of peeled green chile or your favorite chile relish on each tortilla. Fold over as you would a turnover, and pin top with toothpicks to hold together. Fry or grill them in buttered skillet to desired crispness, turning often. Make sure the cheese is melted. Pieces of cooked chicken or turkey, or of leftover meats may be used for filling the *quesadillas*. They are also good with vegetables, tuna, or shrimp. They may be served for lunch, brunch, or snacks. They may be filled ahead of time and grilled when ready to serve. Delicious served with refried beans.

NOTE: If tortillas are not used while still warm, or you are using frozen ones, they should be heated over flame in order to soften them and make them pliable.

QUESADILLITAS

(Little Quesadillas)

Sheer heaven, these. At least that's what my friends are kind enough to say. And do you know, I really do agree!

1 pound fresh masa
½ cup sifted flour
3 tablespoons shortening
1 teaspoon salt

Monterey Jack, American,
*   or Cheddar cheese*
Oil for frying

Mix masa, flour, shortening, and salt until smooth. Shape into balls the size of a large walnut. Pat balls between moistened palms of hands until they are the size of a small, thin pancake, about 3 inches across. Place a generous piece of cheese in the center of each round, fold like a turnover, pinch edges firmly to seal. Fry in deep hot oil until golden brown. Serve at once. Makes about 12 or 15 quesadillitas. These may be served with refried beans, or as a soup or salad accompaniment. If they are made very small they may be served as hors d'oeuvres. They freeze very well.

CHILAQUILES DE JOCOQUI

(Sour Cream and Tortilla Casserole)

This is another versatile dish. I sometimes vary it by adding fried chorizo, another time, ripe olives. And once in awhile I make it with enchilada sauce instead of this one.

12 tortillas, cut in eighths   *Oil for frying*

Sauce:

2 tablespoons oil	*Salt*
1 medium-sized onion, chopped	*½ cup grated Parmesan or Romano cheese*
1 (No. 2½) can solid-pack tomatoes, chopped	*½ pound Monterey Jack or American cheese, cubed*
Salsa Jalapeña, or chile powder, to taste	*1 pint sour cream*
1 teaspoon orégano, rubbed between palms of hands	*Coarsely-grated American cheese*

Fry tortillas lightly and drain on absorbent paper. For the sauce, wilt onion in hot oil; add tomatoes, salsa Jalapeña, orégano, and salt. Cook for 10 to 15 minutes. Set aside. Butter a 2-quart casserole and place alternately layers of tortillas, sauce, Parmesan or Romano cheese, Monterey cheese, and sour cream. Repeat until all ingredients have been used, ending with a layer of sour cream. Bake at 325°F. for 30 to 40 minutes. During the last ten minutes of baking, sprinkle with grated American cheese. Serves 6 to 8.

ENCHILADAS DEL SUR

(Enchiladas from the South)

These are from Sonora.

2 cups sifted flour	½ cup lukewarm water
1 teaspoon salt	Oil for frying
1¼ cup shortening	

Sauce:

1 tablespoon oil	Salt
1 medium-sized onion, chopped	1 pound chorizo
¼ cup chopped green pepper	1 medium-sized onion, chopped
3 cups tomato sauce or purée	¼ pound Monterey Jack cheese, cut in small strips
2 teaspoons chile powder	

Sift flour and salt into a bowl. Mix in the shortening until well distributed, then add water and mix thoroughly. Roll out on floured board and knead about 50 strokes to smooth and round up dough. Roll out to $\frac{1}{16}$-inch thickness. Cut into small tortillas with a 2-inch biscuit cutter and fry until golden brown in just enough oil to cover bottom of skillet. Set aside. Keep warm. *For the sauce:* Wilt onion and green pepper in oil. Add tomato sauce or purée, chile powder, and salt. Cook for 10 minutes, or until well blended. Set aside. Remove chorizo from casing, fry, and add onion, without added fat, until chorizo is well done. Dip tortillas in the sauce, one at a time, and place a layer of them on a platter, then a layer of chorizo mixture and one of cheese. Repeat until all tortillas and chorizo have been used. Thicken remaining sauce with a little flour, if desired. Bring to a boil and pour over enchiladas. Serves 8.

ENCHILADAS DE CHORIZO

(Chorizo Enchiladas)

12 tortillas   *Oil for frying*

Filling:

1 pound chorizo   *3 hard-cooked eggs, sliced*
1 large onion, minced   *3 tablespoons grated Parme-*
1 quart enchilada sauce   *san or American cheese*
*   (page 150)*   *Radishes, sliced or in*
24 pitted ripe olives   *rosettes*

Remove chorizo from casing and fry without added fat. When it starts to brown, add onion and cook until onion is wilted. Set aside and keep warm. Dip tortillas in enchilada sauce, one at a time, and fry lightly in oil. Put some chorizo mixture, 2 olives, and some cheese on each tortilla. Roll and arrange on a hot platter. Pour the remaining sauce (which may be thickened with a little flour, if desired) over them. Sprinkle with cheese and serve garnished with egg and radishes. Chopped lettuce may be served with this, too, and there you have a complete meal. Serves 6 or 12.

ENCHILADAS DE ACAPULCO

(Enchiladas, Acapulco Style)

12 tortillas

Filling:

3 cups cubed, cooked
    chicken, turkey, or veal
1 cup chopped ripe olives
½ cup blanched and
    chopped almonds
½ cup minced green onions
    Salt

1 quart enchilada sauce
    (page 150) or canned
    sauce
1 cup grated Parmesan or
    American cheese
Sour cream

Mix meat with olives, almonds, onions, and salt. Set aside. Heat sauce and drop tortillas into it, one at a time, allowing them to stand until soaked and heated. Remove from sauce. Place a generous amount of the filling on each tortilla and roll. Arrange on a large platter, folded side down, pour sauce over them and sprinkle with half of the cheese. Serve at once. Put remaining cheese in a bowl and take to the table, along with bowls of additional finely chopped green onions and sour cream. Serves 6 or 12.

ENCHILADAS TAMPIQUEÑAS

(Enchiladas, Tampico Style)

Note that these are folded and not rolled. Just to show that the Mexicans aren't creatures of habit.

8 tortillas
    Oil for frying
¼ pound Monterey Jack
    cheese, cubed
½ pint sour cream

3 cups chile chipotle sauce
    (page 168)
Ripe olives
Hard-cooked egg, sliced

Fry tortillas lightly in oil. Place cheese, sour cream, and sauce on each one and fold over like a turnover. Arrange in shallow baking dish, spoon remaining sauce and sour cream over them and bake at 325°F. for 15 or 20 minutes. Serve garnished with olives and slices of egg. Serves 4 or 8.

ENFRIJOLADAS

(Bean Enchiladas)

These enchiladas may also be filled with fried chorizo, leftover meats, or cheese. They make a complete meal, served with a green tossed salad.

18 tortillas

Oil for frying

Bean sauce:

2 cups pink beans, soaked
    overnight
2 quarts water

2 tablespoons bacon
    drippings or lard
2 tablespoons minced onion
    Salt

Filling:

2 tablespoons butter or
    margarine
1 medium-sized onion,
    minced
1½ cups solid-pack tomatoes

2 tablespoons salsa Jalapeña,
    or your favorite chile
    relish
3 cups cubed, cooked chicken
    Salt
1 pint sour cream, salted

Wash beans, drain, and add water and salt. Cook until well done. Mash thoroughly with potato masher. Heat bacon drippings in skillet, add onion and wilt, add mashed beans and cook over slow fire, stirring often to prevent sticking. They should be thick, but not dry. *For the filling:* Wilt onion in butter. Add tomatoes, chile relish, and salt and cook a few minutes before adding chicken. Fry tortillas lightly in oil. Put some of the filling in each one, fold over like a turnover and place in shallow glass baking dish. When all tortillas and filling are used, cover with the bean mixture and spoon sour cream over all. Bake at 350°F. for about 15 or 20 minutes. Serves 9 or 18.

TOSTADAS DE POLLO

(Chicken Tostadas)

12 tostadas (page 127)

Filling:

1 tablespoon oil	*Salt*
1 small onion, chopped	*1 cup cooked, cut string beans*
1 large tomato, peeled and chopped, or 1 cup solid-pack tomatoes	*Shredded lettuce, with oil, vinegar and salt added, if desired*
2 cups cooked, cubed chicken	*Avocado*
Salsa Jalapeña, or your favorite Mexican chile sauce, to taste	*Green stuffed olives*

Wilt onion in hot oil. Add tomato and cook a few minutes. Add chicken, chile relish, and salt and mix well. Cover tostadas with some of this filling. Arrange string beans on top, then lettuce. Garnish with wedges of avocado and thin slices of olives. Delightful served with refried beans. Any tostada sauce may be added to these if you want them more moist. Serves 6 or 12.

TOSTADAS DE FRIJOL Y CHORIZO

(Tostadas with Refried Beans and Chorizo)

12 tostadas
2 cups refried beans (page 114)
¾ pound chorizo
1 small onion, chopped
2 cups tostada sauce, #1 (page 165)

3 tablespoons grated Parmesan cheese
Shredded lettuce
Avocado
Radishes
Cucumber

Cover tostadas with hot beans. Remove chorizo from casing and fry without added fat. When it starts to brown, add onion and cook a few minutes longer. Now spread this over the beans, sprinkle on the cheese, and cover all with lettuce. Garnish with avocado wedges, thin slices of radishes and slices of cucumber, which have been marinated in oil, vinegar, and salt. Serves 6 or 12.

TOSTADAS DE GUACAMOLE

(Guacamole Tostadas)

12 tostadas
3 cups guacamole (page 8)
2 cups cubed, cooked chicken, preferably white meat

Shredded lettuce
Radish rosettes

Cover tostadas with guacamole. Arrange chicken on top and garnish with lettuce and radish rosettes. Serves 6 or 12.

TOSTADAS TAPATIAS

(Tostadas, Tapatia Style)

When making these *tostadas* I have everything prepared before serving time. I keep the various ingredients in bowls so that I can easily assemble the dish at the last minute. They are a real favorite with the men, bless them!

12 tostadas
 2 cups hot refried beans
    (page 114)
 3 tablespoons grated
    Parmesan cheese
    Shredded lettuce, with oil,
    vinegar, and salt added to
    it, if desired

1 (9 oz.) jar semi-boneless
    pigs' feet
    Avocado wedges
    Radish rosettes
    Onion rings
2 cups tostada sauce, #1
    (page 165)

Place a layer of beans on each tostada; sprinkle with cheese and cover with lettuce. Garnish with pigs' feet, wedges of avocado, radish rosettes, and onion rings. Pour sauce over all. Sauce may be hot or cold. Serves 6 or 12.

TOSTADAS DE VIGILIA

(Tostadas for Lent)

Who minds Lent when there are dishes like this to enjoy?

6 tostadas
1 (7 oz.) can solid-pack tuna
1 tablespoon minced onion
2 peeled green chiles, chopped
2 tablespoons wine vinegar
1 cup sliced, cooked zucchini

1 cup tostada sauce #1 (page 165)
Shredded lettuce
Cubes of cucumber
Avocado wedges

Empty tuna, oil and all, in a bowl and break up with a fork. Mix well with onion, chiles, and vinegar. Spread this mixture on tostadas; place slices of zucchini on top, then lettuce. Garnish with cucumbers marinated in oil, vinegar, and salt, and wedges of avocado. Pour chilled sauce over all. Serves 3 or 6.

TOSTADAS CON JOCOQUI Y CHILE VERDE

(Tostadas with Sour Cream and Green Chile)

Simple and simply wonderful!

12 tostadas
3 cups hot refried beans
    (page 114)
¼ cup grated Parmesan or
    Romano cheese

1 pint sour cream
1 can peeled green chiles
Salt

Spread hot beans on tostadas. Sprinkle with cheese. Mix sour cream with chiles and salt and spread on top of beans. Serve at once. If you like tostadas more spicy, add some green chile relish to the sour cream. Serves 6 or 12.

TOSTADAS ESTILO TAMAULIPAS

(Tostadas, Tamaulipas Style)

Here, again, pigs' feet add their special touch, and also, here again, I prepare everything ahead of time and assemble at serving time.

12 tostadas

Filling:

1 pound chorizo	*Shredded lettuce, seasoned*
1 medium-sized onion,	*with salt, vinegar and oil,*
chopped	*if desired*
1 cup cubed, cooked potatoes	*1 (9 oz.) jar semi-boneless*
1 chayote, or zucchini,	*pigs' feet*
cooked and cubed	*12 pickled wax peppers*
1 cup cooked peas	*2 cups tostada sauce, #1*
Salt	*(page 165), hot or cold*

Remove chorizo from casing and fry without added fat. When it starts to brown, add onion, cook a few minutes longer before adding potatoes, chayote, and peas. Place some of this filling on top of each tostada; cover with shredded lettuce, garnish with pigs' feet and one pepper in center of each tostada. Pour sauce over all. Serves 6 or 12.

TOSTADAS DE SARDINAS

(Sardine Tostadas)

Mexicans are very fond of sardines. This, too, is probably a throw-back to the Spaniards.

12 tostadas

Filling:

1 tablespoon oil	*3 tablespoons grated Parmesan*
1 small onion, chopped	*cheese*
1 large tomato, peeled and	*Shredded lettuce seasoned*
chopped	*with salt, vinegar and oil,*
1 cup fried beans (page 113)	*if desired*
1 (3¾ oz.) can sardines in	*Chile chipotle sauce (page*
oil, boned and shredded	*168)*
	Radishes

Wilt onion in hot oil; add tomato and beans; cook until thick, but not dry. Add sardines just before removing from stove. Cover each tostada with some of this filling; sprinkle with cheese; top with lettuce and pour sauce over all. Serve garnished with thin slices of radishes. Serves 6 or 12.

GORDITAS

(Little Fat Tortillas)

These are as endearing as their name. Their shape is enchanting, their flavor delectable! *Chalupas* are exactly the same except they are shaped like the little boats (*chalupa*) that are used in the floating gardens of Xochimilco.

1 pound fresh masa
½ cup sifted flour
3 tablespoons shortening

1 teaspoon salt
Chorizo and grated cheese

Green Chile Sauce:

1½ cups tomato purée
1 onion, finely chopped
1½ teaspoons salt
1 teaspoon orégano

1 tablespoon vinegar
2 tablespoons oil
Peeled green chiles, to taste

Place masa, flour, shortening, and salt in a bowl, and mix until smooth. Shape dough into balls the size of large walnuts, then pat each one between moistened palms of hands until they are the size of small pancakes (about 3 inches across). Cook on both sides in an ungreased heavy skillet. While still hot, pinch up edges between thumb and fingers to form a border, and pinch up a small amount in the center so that they look like *sombreros*. Set aside until ready to serve, and make the sauce.

Sauce: Place all ingredients in a saucepan, stir to combine well, and simmer over moderate heat for about 20 minutes, or until onion is cooked and sauce thoroughly blended. Serve cold.

Just before serving, fry cakes in hot oil until golden brown and drain on absorbent paper. Arrange on a large serving platter and fill brim of each little hat with fried chorizo. Sprinkle generously with grated cheese and pile shredded lettuce on top. Pour a little cold sauce over each one and serve with radish rings and refried beans. Makes about 12 or 15 gorditas.

TORTOLETAS MEXICANAS

(Mexican Tarts)

¼ pound fresh masa
2 cups sifted flour
2 tablespoons lard or
shortening

2 tablespoons sour cream
1 teaspoon salt
2 eggs
Oil for frying

Filling:

3 chorizos (½ pound)
1 medium-sized onion,
chopped
3 cups cooked pink beans,
partially mashed

¼ cup sour cream
Salt to taste
Radishes
Avocado
Monterey Jack cheese

Mix masa, flour, lard, sour cream, and salt until well blended. Add eggs, one at a time, stirring after each addition. Divide dough into 8 pieces and shape each piece into a *tortoleta,* by first making a pancake about 4-inches in diameter and ¼-inch thick. Press edges of pancake between fingers making a rim around the edge and forming a little cup. Fry in hot oil, at least 1½ inches deep, until golden brown. Set aside to drain on absorbent paper. *To make filling:* Remove chorizos from skin, crumble, and fry without added fat for a few minutes. Add onion and fry until onion is soft, add beans, sour cream, and salt and cook until bubbly hot. Fill each *tortoleta* with this filling. Garnish with slices of radishes, avocado wedges, and cheese. Serve hot. Serves 8.

TAMAL DE CAZUELA CON CHILE COLORADO

(Tamale Pie with Red Chile Sauce)

And here's another casserole made with masa. If you can't find any, drain canned whole hominy, grind three times, and knead well until pliable. It's not the same but it's better than corn meal.

½ *pound lard*
1½ *pounds fresh masa*
2 *teaspoons salt*

2 *teaspoons baking powder*
½ *cup chicken broth*

Filling:

2 *tablespoons oil*
2 *cups enchilada sauce*
   (*page 150*)
1 (8 oz.) *can tomato sauce*
   Salt

2 *cups cooked, cubed*
   chicken, beef, or pork
1 *tablespoon grated*
   Parmesan cheese

Beat lard to the consistency of whipped cream. Gradually add masa alternately with the broth, then salt and baking powder. Continue beating until the mixture is so light and fluffy that when a little of it is dropped in a cup of cold water, it will come to the top. *To make the filling:* Heat oil, add enchilada sauce, tomato sauce, and salt. Add chicken and simmer until chicken is well coated with the sauce. Spread the bottom of a 2-quart casserole with half of the masa mixture. Spoon chicken filling on top, reserving one cup of the sauce. Cover with the rest of the masa and bake in a 350°F. oven for one hour. About 15 minutes before it's done, sprinkle cheese on top and continue baking. The extra cup of sauce may be used when serving, for those who like a more moist pie. This pie can be frozen. Serves 4 to 6.

NOTE: If you are using a prepared enchilada sauce, it should be thickened.

Salsas

❦ (Sauces)

Mexico, like France, is a land of sauces, but they are as different as the two languages. Whereas the French use much butter, cream, and egg yolk, the Mexicans are more apt to use vegetables, particularly chile and the tomato. Some are hot, some are not. All are very flavorsome. They are a very important part of the Mexican cuisine as many dishes depend upon the addition of a sauce for their completion.

SALSA DE PEREJIL

(Parsley Sauce)

I can't think of anything that this cold sauce wouldn't be good on, though it's usually served with fish, tongue, boiled beef, or cauliflower. Try it on brains, too, and on sliced tomatoes and/or a vegetable salad.

½ *cup finely minced parsley*　　3 *tablespoons vinegar*
¼ *cup almonds, blanched and*　⅓ *cup olive oil*
　　chopped　　　　　　　　　　*Salt*

Combine all ingredients and mix well. Serve cold with fish, tongue, boiled beef, or cauliflower. Makes about 1 cup.

SALSA DE CHILE COLORADO

(Red Chile Sauce)

Here is my version of that indispensable Mexican chile sauce. I have Americanized it a little, as I have noted below.

Since some chiles are not as hot as others, you may want to add some chile tepines to suit your taste. My personal touch is adding the tomato sauce, as it is not the Mexican custom to do so. I happen to like it better that way. In making this sauce, Mexicans do not thicken it; but you may do so, after dipping tortillas, if desired. What's more, if you do not care to go through all this trouble, there are several good prepared enchilada sauces on the market. This sauce may be used for enchiladas, cooked chicken, beef or pork.

6 *chiles pasillas*　　　　　　　1 *tablespoon vinegar*
6 *chiles colorados*　　　　　　1 *can tomato sauce*
3 *cups hot water or stock*　　　　(*optional*)
2 *cloves garlic*　　　　　　　　2 *tablespoons oil*
1 *teaspoon orégano*　　　　　　*Salt*
¼ *teaspoon comino*

Put chiles in hot, dry skillet until parched. Remove seeds; wash and soak chiles in hot water for 15 to 20 minutes, or until soft. Do not discard water. Add remaining ingredients except oil and mix in blender or grind until very smooth; strain if necessary. Heat oil, add sauce and simmer for about 10 minutes to blend flavors. Makes about 1 quart, enough for 12 enchiladas.

SALSA DE CHÍCHARO Y TOMATE

(Peas and Tomato Sauce)

This sauce is a conversation piece as no one can guess what's in it. As I remember, it's a lovely green color, and the flavor is piquant—in spots. And if you don't know what I am talking about, just try it.

1 medium-sized onion	¼ teaspoon thyme
1 cup cooked peas	3 finely-chopped pickled wax
3 tomatoes, finely chopped	peppers
1 tablespoon capers	1 tablespoon oil
12 olives, sliced	3 tablespoons vinegar
½ teaspoon orégano	

Combine onions and peas in blender (or finely chop onion and sieve peas). Add remaining ingredients; mix in blender. Serve this sauce cold with fish, tongue, or veal. Makes about 2 cups.

SALSA PARA TOSTADAS Y TACOS #1

(Sauce for Tostadas and Tacos #1)

This sauce should be hot—at least to be Mexican—so add the green chiles or chile chipotle to suit your taste.

2 (8 oz.) cans thin tomato sauce	1 tablespoon oil
	1 tablespoon vinegar
Green peeled chiles, chopped, or	¼ teaspoon orégano, rubbed between palms of hands
Chile chipotle, chopped to taste	Salt

Mix all ingredients well. This sauce may be served hot or cold. Makes about 1 pint.

SALSA PARA TOSTADAS Y TACOS #2

(Sauce for Tostadas and Tacos #2)

Here's another sauce for tostadas and tacos—you may prefer it to the first one.

4 large tomatoes, peeled and chopped, or 1 (No. 2½) can solid-pack tomatoes, chopped

1 medium-sized onion, or 1 bunch green onions, chopped

2 tablespoons chopped fresh cilantro, or

1 teaspoon coriander seeds, mashed

1 tablespoon oil

1 tablespoon wine vinegar

Peeled green chiles, to taste, chopped, or your favorite chile relish

Salt

Combine all ingredients and mix well. If you use coriander seeds, they should be soaked in a tablespoon of hot water and this water strained into the sauce. This could also be made with 1 teaspoon orégano, rubbed between palms of the hands, in place of coriander. May be served hot or cold. Makes almost 1 quart sauce.

SALSA DE TOMATILLO

(Tomatillo Sauce)

The flavor of the tomatillo is an exotic one that most people like very much. It tastes more like a green tomato than anything else I can think of. It's a very favorite flavor with me.

1 small onion, minced
2 tablespoons oil
4 cans tomatillo (available in
   Mexican stores)
2 cloves garlic, mashed or
   pressed

2 cans peeled green chiles or
   your favorite Mexican
   green chile sauce
Pinch of sugar
Salt

Wilt onion in hot oil. Sieve or blend tomatillo. Add to onion, with liquid from cans. Add garlic, chiles, sugar, and salt. Cook for about 15 or 20 minutes, or until slightly thickened. This yields 1 quart of sauce.

SALSA DE AGUACATE

(Avocado Dressing)

This dressing is much lower in calories than most salad dressings, but doesn't taste at all like a diet dish.

2 medium-sized ripe
   avocados
2 tablespoons lime or lemon
   juice
1½ tablespoons
   finely-chopped onion

1 small clove garlic, crushed or
   pressed
1 small can hot green chile
   pepper (optional)
1 teaspoon salt
1 ripe tomato, peeled and
   chopped

Cut avocados in half, remove seeds and skin. Put avocados, lime juice, onion, garlic, chile pepper, and salt in electric blender and blend until well mixed (or mash all thoroughly together). Stir in tomato, chill in refrigerator until ready to use. This mixture will keep its color because of lemon or lime juice, which is a help. Serve as dressing for cooked or raw vegetables, such as cauliflower, carrots, tomatoes, green beans, or on any salad. Makes about 1 pint.

SALSA RANCHERA

(Ranch-style Sauce)

Here's another good-on-anything sauce. But go easy with the chiles serranos. They are HOT!

1 teaspoon cilantro
  (coriander) seeds, crushed
2 cups solid-pack tomatoes
1 small onion, chopped

1 clove garlic
2 or more chiles serranos
  (available in Mexican
  stores)

Soak cilantro seeds in hot water for 5 minutes. Strain. Combine cilantro water with tomatoes, onions, garlic, and chiles and mix in electric blender. Add salt. This sauce may be used cold or hot. Good for meats and poultry, tostadas, tacos, and fried eggs. Makes about 1 pint.

SALSA DE CHILE CHIPOTLE

(Chile Chipotle Sauce)

It is well worth looking up a Mexican store to get the chile chipotles as they give this sauce a distinctive and delightful flavor. Use it wherever a chile sauce is indicated.

2 tablespoons oil
1 medium-sized onion,
  chopped
2 cloves garlic, mashed or
  pressed

1 (No. 2½) can solid-pack
  tomatoes, chopped
1 can tomato sauce
1 or more chopped chile
  chipotle
Salt to taste

Wilt onion in hot oil, add all other ingredients and cook for 15 or 20 minutes. This will yield 1 quart of sauce.

SALSA DE PIÑÓN PARA PEZCADO FRIO

(Pine Nut Sauce for Cold Fish)

Try this on a simple shrimp salad. I'll promise that you'll get raves!

3 ounces pine nuts (½ cup) 1 cup whipping cream
3 hard-cooked egg yolks Salt and pepper

Combine all ingredients and mix in a blender. Or grind pine nuts and egg yolks in a food grinder, whip the cream, combine and season. Makes about 1½ cups sauce.

SALSA VERDE

(Green Sauce)

This is typical of Mexican sauces at their best. I like to serve it on chicken, fish, or tongue.

2 tablespoons pumpkin seeds 3 cups chicken broth
1 can green peeled chiles ¼ cup oil
¾ cup chopped parsley Salt and pepper

Toast pumpkin seeds until browned or use toasted pumpkin seeds, called pepitas, and grind with the chiles and parsley until very fine. Put through the grinder twice if necessary, or whirl in blender. Add a little of the chicken broth and strain. Add the strained mixture and remaining broth to the hot oil, heat thoroughly and serve. Makes almost 1 quart.

SALSA LUISA

(Sauce Louise)

Luisa Loshuertos, my darling mother, created this sauce. I use it often.

¼ *cup butter*
1 *small onion, finely*
  chopped
½ *cup flour*
⅛ *teaspoon nutmeg*
2½ *cups chicken broth*

Salt and pepper
3 *egg yolks, slightly beaten*
2 *tablespoons butter*
2 *tablespoons strained lemon*
  juice

Place the butter and onion in a saucepan and cook until onion is soft but not browned. Then blend in the flour, nutmeg, broth, and salt and pepper. Cook until mixture is thickened and smooth, stirring frequently, about 10 minutes. Turn heat very low and beat in the egg yolks, 2 tablespoons of butter, and lemon juice. Cook 2 or 3 minutes longer. Remove from heat and stir briskly to smooth sauce. Serve over any cooked vegetable such as asparagus, broccoli, carrots, or cauliflower. Sauce may be well covered and stored under refrigeration for several days, if desired. This makes about 1 pint.

SALSA DE ALMENDRAS

(Almond Sauce)

Everyone loves almonds in Mexico just as they do here. This sauce is wonderful on breaded veal cutlets, sautéed chicken or rabbit, and boiled tongue.

3 tablespoons oil

½ cup almonds

1 slice bread

1 clove garlic

2 tablespoons minced onion

¼ cup tomato sauce

1½ cups chicken broth

Salt and pepper

Fry almonds and bread in hot oil until browned; add garlic long enough to wilt. Remove mixture from oil, cool, and grind to consistency of paste. Dilute with a little broth. Set aside. Wilt onion in the same oil, add tomato sauce, remaining broth, salt and pepper and almond mixture. Simmer from 5 to 10 minutes. Makes about 1 pint.

SALSA DE PIMIENTOS PARA PEZCADO FRIO

(Pimiento Sauce for Cold Fish)

When I use this as a dressing on wedges of lettuce, I always add a dash of lemon juice or wine vinegar. It's also good on fish salad as well as on cold fish.

1 can pimientos

4 hard-cooked egg yolks

1 cup heavy cream

Salt and pepper

10 stuffed olives, thinly sliced

1 tablespoon lemon juice

Combine pimientos, egg yolks, cream, salt, and pepper in a blender, or grind pimientos and egg yolks in a food grinder and combine with cream, salt, and pepper. Add olives and lemon juice. Makes about 2 cups sauce.

Empanadas

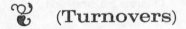 **(Turnovers)**

Empanadas are Mexican turnovers and they are great favorites on both sides of the border. They may have either sweet or savory fillings. When made in miniature size, they are called *empanaditas* and are delightful with tea or cocktails. They freeze beautifully, either before or after filling. When frozen, uncooked, be sure to thaw before baking or frying. I like them best when fried but I admit they are lower in calories when baked. But that's life!

EMPANADAS (BASIC RECIPE)

(Mexican Turnovers)

2 cups sifted all-purpose flour | ½ cup shortening
2 teaspoons baking powder | ⅓ cup of ice water
1 teaspoon salt | (approximately)

Sift together into a bowl, flour, baking powder, and salt; add the shortening and work into flour as you would for pastry, adding enough ice water to hold dough together. Divide into 12 even pieces. Roll out each piece to make a round about 3- to 4-inches in diameter. Place a spoonful of filling on one half of each round, wet the edges with water, and fold the other half over, pressing the edges firmly to seal in the filling. For fillings, see page 178. Fry the empanadas in hot oil until golden brown and drain on absorbent paper; or bake for 15 to 20 minutes at 400°F. Makes 12 empanadas.

EMPANADAS DE MARUJA

(Maruja's Turnovers)

Maruja Palm, married to a Swede, is a Mexican friend of long standing. She showed me this easy trick and I adore it. Next time you want to make a quick pastry, forget your mixes and try this.

1 cup sifted all-purpose flour *⅔ cup whipping cream*
½ teaspoon salt

Sift flour and salt together, stir in whipping cream to make a stiff dough. Roll out on floured board to ⅛-inch thickness. Cut into circles with a 2-inch cookie cutter. Fill with anchovy paste, liver paté, cheese, or your favorite spread made from tuna, shrimp, crab, or ham. Fold over like a turnover and fry in hot fat until golden brown on both sides and serve immediately. Makes about 2½ dozen.

NOTE: These can be made larger and served as an entree. They may be fried, stored in freezer and when ready to use, heated in a 375°F. oven for 4 to 5 minutes. These empanadas should not be baked because they are much better fried.

EMPANADAS DE QUESO DE CREMA

(Cream Cheese Empanadas)

This recipe for pastry is so easy and good that I make it often. It's good for sweet empanadas, too. It's an old one, but it's amazing how many people don't know it.

1 (3 oz.) package cream cheese	½ cup butter
	1 cup flour

Cream the butter and cheese together until blended. Add flour and work into a ball. Refrigerate dough overnight and remove from refrigerator ½ hour before using. Roll out dough, cut in rounds about an inch in diameter, fill, and bake at 400°F. for 10 to 12 minutes. These empanadas are nice served with salads, soups, or as appetizers. Anchovy paste, deviled ham, or a mixture of butter and grated cheese make good fillings. Makes about two dozen.

EMPANADAS DE JAIBA

(Crab Empanadas)

Use recipe for empanadas #1 (page 173).

Filling:

1 tablespoon butter or margarine	½ pound cooked crab
	1 tablespoon minced parsley
1 medium-sized onion, minced	1 (3 oz.) jar pimiento-stuffed olives, chopped
1 large tomato, peeled and chopped	1 teaspoon lemon juice
	Salt and pepper

Wilt onion in butter or margarine, add tomato and cook a few minutes. Add crab, parsley, olives, lemon juice, salt and pepper. Mix well and fill empanadas. Bake or fry. Serve hot with a side salad of shredded lettuce seasoned with oil, vinegar, salt and pepper. Garnish with radish roses. Filling is enough for 12 medium-sized turnovers.

EMPANADAS CORDOBESAS

(Mexican Turnovers, Cordova Style)

What a fine supper dish these make served with a simple salad and some good Mexican beer, for those who enjoy it. I roll it like pie crust and cut the circles out with a cookie cutter. And then, I want you to know, mine are as pretty as anyone else's.

Pie crust (basis 2 cups flour,
*   add 1 teaspoon chile*
*   powder to pastry)*

Filling:

1 tablespoon oil	Salt and pepper
2 onions, minced	1 tablespoon flour
2 tomatoes, chopped	½ cup broth
1 tablespoon chopped	12 or 15 pitted green olives
pimiento	2 hard-cooked eggs, chopped
2 pounds cooked beef, cut in	fine
small cubes	½ cup raisins
1 large cooked potato, cut in	
small cubes	

Wilt onion in hot oil; add tomatoes and pimiento and cook for a few minutes; then add meat and potatoes, seasoned with salt and pepper. Dissolve flour in cold broth and add to meat mixture. Cook until it thickens, then cool. Add olives, eggs, and raisins. Mix well.

Divide pastry into 12 even pieces. Roll out each piece to make a round about 3- to 5-inches in diameter. Place filling on one half of each round; wet the edges with water and fold the other half over, pressing the edges firmly to seal in the filling. Bake empanadas 15 to 20 minutes at 400°F. Makes 12 empanadas.

EMPANADAS DE DULCE

(Sweet Turnovers)

Americans think these sweet empanadas are good for dessert or, when made small, to serve with tea. They are also fine for buffets or picnics as the small ones are a finger food.

2 cups all-purpose flour	½ cup shortening
2 tablespoons sugar	⅓ cup ice water
2 teaspoons baking powder	1 cup sugar
1 teaspoon salt	1 tablespoon cinnamon

Sift flour, baking powder, sugar, and salt into a bowl; work into this the shortening as you would for pastry; add ice water, using only enough to hold dough together. Divide dough into 12 even-sized pieces. Roll out on floured board to make rounds about 3- to 4-inches in diameter. Place a spoonful of one of the following fillings on one half of each round: Thick applesauce flavored with cinnamon; any flavor jelly or jam; or French custard cream. Fold the other half of the pastry over the filled half, wetting the edges and pressing firmly to seal in the filling. Fry in deep hot oil until golden brown and drain on absorbent paper. These empanadas can also be baked in a 400°F. oven for 15 to 20 minutes. While they are still hot, dip them in a mixture of 1 cup sugar and 1 tablespoon cinnamon. Makes 12 empanadas.

RELLENOS PARA EMPANADAS DE DULCE

(Fillings for Sweet Empanadas)

1. Crushed pineapple with grated coconut.
2. Mashed sweet potatoes with pineapple and almonds.
3. Mashed sweet potatoes with coconut.
4. Mashed sweet potatoes with coconut and pineapple.
5. Fruit preserves of any kind.
6. Cream cheese and quince paste.
7. Applesauce with cinnamon and nuts.

RELLENOS PARA EMPANADAS

(Mexican Turnover Fillings)

Here are some suggestions for empanada fillings. Of course, you can use almost anything, so make up your own. The only trick is to have them well seasoned.

Cooked chicken, pimientos and stuffed olives, chopped. Add capers and a small amount of grated Swiss cheese.

Chicken livers in Sherry sauce (page 214).

Cooked chicken, blanched almonds and raisins, chopped. Add chile chipotle, chopped, or your favorite Mexican chile sauce and a raw egg. Mix well.

Cooked, chopped chicken with mushroom pieces and a little mayonnaise.

Cooked, chopped chicken, fresh tomato, peeled and cut in tiny pieces, and chopped peeled green chiles.

Cooked, chopped spinach or Swiss chard, fried chorizo, and chile chipotle, chopped, or your favorite chile relish.

Cooked spinach or Swiss chard, cooked ham, and some raisins, all chopped. Add pine nuts and a little melted butter.

Carne de Puerco con chile verde (page 90), with the meat cut in tiny pieces.

Shrimps, canned or fresh, hard-cooked egg, and pimientos, all chopped.

Bacalao a la Vizcaina (page 52). Be sure to drain tomato sauce from it.

Shredded tuna, sardines, or salmon with chopped green onion, lemon juice, chopped hard-cooked egg and a little mayonnaise.

Cooked, chopped zucchini or Swiss chard with fresh tomatoes, peeled and cut in tiny pieces; chopped green onions and peeled green chiles, little pieces of Monterey Jack or Cheddar cheese.

Refried beans sprinkled with grated cheese and strips of green chile.

Leftover chopped meats or deviled ham with cheese and/or chile.

Legumbres

ℰ (Vegetables)

Vegetables, like so many other Mexican dishes, are usually cooked in combination with other things. Take peas, for instance. I don't even include them in this vegetable section because they are used mostly in rice, meat dishes, and soups, rather than alone. However, Mexicans do serve them in cream sauce (believe it or not!) and sometimes they boil them with mint in the water.

ESPÁRRAGOS CON SALSA LUISA

(Asparagus with Sauce Louise)

Clean asparagus well and break off tough part of stems. Cook, covered with boiling salted water, from 6 to 10 minutes depending upon thickness of the stalks. Do not overcook, as the asparagus should be tender but firm, not droopy. Serve with Salsa Luisa (page 170).

PIMIENTOS FRESCOS VERDES O COLORADOS

(Fresh Green or Red Peppers)

This recipe may be made of green *or* red peppers or green *and* red peppers. The latter look very gay indeed, but both taste wonderful!

Place peppers under broiler flame until blistered all over. That means you'll have to turn them once or twice. Put them in a heavy paper bag and close tightly so that they can steam for 20 minutes. Then peel off skins, remove seeds and core, and cut in strips. Rub a serving bowl with garlic, arrange peppers in it and cover with oil, vinegar, salt, and pepper to taste. Let stand in the refrigerator for a few hours before serving. How many peppers? How many do you have?

BOLAS DE PAPA DE LUJO

(Luxurious Potato Balls)

Every one of my friends likes these potato balls. I find that they go beautifully with almost any roasted or broiled meat or poultry, or with broiled fish.

3 medium-sized baked
    potatoes
½ cup water
2 tablespoons butter

½ cup flour
2 eggs
Salt and pepper to taste

Scoop potatoes from shells while hot, and mash smooth. Measure out 2 cups of potatoes, loosely packed, and to them add this batter: Boil water with butter, add flour all at once, and mix well until it separates from sides of pan. Add unbeaten eggs, one at a time, beat well, and season after mixing with potatoes. Shape into balls resembling small potatoes, roll in flour, and deep fry in hot oil. If you choose, you may add the 1 tablespoon of chopped parsley and the 2 tablespoons of grated Parmesan called for in the soup version of these. These freeze nicely. Makes 18 to 20 balls.

PERITAS DE PAPA

(Little Potato Pears)

Here's a way a potato can masquerade as fruit. Mexicans are full of such little tricks! Use them as a garnish or just served as potatoes. They are decorative, I am sure.

2 cups mashed potatoes	1 egg yolk
½ cup coarsely grated Swiss cheese	¼ cup fine bread crumbs
1 whole egg	Salt
	Oil for frying

Mix all ingredients well and shape into "pears." Fry in deep fat or oil until brown. When cool, put a whole clove at the tip of each "pear." Yields from 12 to 15.

CALABAZA ENMIELADA

(Banana Squash with Brown Sugar)

This squash dish is sweet, as you'll guess when you read the recipe. A typical Mexican way of serving this is to scoop the cooked squash into a deep bowl, pouring the syrup over the top and adding milk. This they like for breakfast.

1 small banana squash (5 to 6 pounds)	1 pound brown sugar
	¼ cup water

Wipe the squash with a damp cloth. Cut into quarters, or smaller pieces, if desired. Remove seeds and pack brown sugar on top of each piece of squash. Place in a pan that can be tightly covered, and pour the water into the pan. Cover and cook on top of stove until tender. After this is done, if the syrup is not thick enough, add more sugar to suit your taste.

TORTAS DE CALABACITAS

(Zucchini Pancakes)

These are delicious cold as well as hot. That's why Mexicans love to take them for *"dias de campo"*—a day of camping. In other words, a picnic.

2 cups (about 1 pound) un-cooked zucchini, grated	1 egg, well beaten
½ cup flour	Salt
1 teaspoon baking powder	Butter for frying

Put zucchini in a bowl; add flour and baking powder sifted together, then add salt and egg, and mix well. Fry in butter as you would pancakes, making each pancake about 2 to 3 inches in diameter. Makes 10 to 12 pancakes.

ESPINACA CON PIMIENTO

(Spinach with Pimiento)

Fry cooked, chopped spinach in olive oil to which garlic has been added. Serve topped with slices of hard-cooked egg and strips of pimientos, or with buttered croutons.

EJOTES CON CHILE VERDE

(String Beans with Green Chile)

Simple? Yes. Good? Yes.

1 pound string beans	*2 peeled green chiles, chopped*
3 tablespoons oil	*1 cup chicken or beef broth*
2 tablespoons minced onion	*Salt*
1 (8 oz.) can tomato sauce	

String and wash beans and cut lengthwise in halves. Wilt onion in hot oil, add tomato sauce, chiles, string beans, broth, and salt. Cover tightly and cook until beans are just tender. A little orégano, rubbed between palms of hands, is a pleasant addition to this. Serves 4.

HABICHUELAS CON HONGOS

(String Beans with Mushrooms)

1 pound string beans	*Salt and pepper*
2 tablespoons olive oil	*1 (4 oz.) can sliced*
2 tablespoons minced onion	*mushrooms*
3 red pimientos, cut in strips	*Slices of hard-cooked egg*
1 tablespoon minced parsley	

Either French-cut or slice beans and cook until just barely tender in boiling, salted water. Fry onion in oil until transparent; add cooked, drained beans, pimientos, and parsley. Fry together lightly, season, and add mushrooms and their liquid. Garnish platter with slices of hard-cooked egg. Serves 4.

CHILE CON QUESO

(Green Chile with Cheese)

Wait until you've tasted this, if you never have. My friends are mad for it and to tell the truth, so am I. It's delightful for breakfast or lunch, with refried beans and tortillas, but it's also wonderful for a cocktail dip, with tostaditas.

1 small onion, minced	½ pound Monterey cream
2 tablespoons butter	cheese, cubed
1 cup solid-pack tomatoes	1 cup cream
1 can peeled green chiles,	Salt and pepper
chopped	

Wilt onion in butter; add tomatoes, chiles, salt and pepper; simmer for 15 minutes, then add cubed cheese. When cheese begins to melt, add cream. Serves 4.

TOMATES FRITOS A LA MEXICANA

(Fried Tomatoes, Mexican Style)

These are strictly delicious! Serve them with rice or toast or tortillas and with refried beans. The recipe came from Monterrey, Mexico, and got into my kitchen through the generosity of *mi querida amiga,* Lillian Couchman.

4 tomatoes, preferably	4 tablespoons butter
beefsteak variety	1 cup whipping cream
2 tablespoons chopped chives	1 tablespoon cornstarch
2 tablespoons minced parsley	Salt and pepper
2 peeled green chiles, chopped	
(more if desired)	

Wash tomatoes and cut in thick slices; lay them on a large glass baking dish, making sure they are not on top of each other; then sprinkle all over with the chives, parsley, and chiles. Allow to stand for at least three hours.

Melt butter in skillet and sauté tomatoes on both sides; make sure all of the chives, parsley and chiles are used too, but do not brown. Season with salt and pepper. Remove to a hot platter. Pour cream into skillet in which tomatoes were fried, thicken with cornstarch, and pour all over the tomatoes. Serves 4.

CALABAZITAS DE MAMÁ

(Mama's Zucchini)

As perhaps you've guessed, my mother was a good cook, too good to need to follow a recipe. Here, for instance, she sometimes used a little leftover, diced ham—say ¼ cup—instead of the bacon.

2 strips uncooked bacon, cut in pieces
1 pound zucchini, cut in slices
1 small onion, chopped
1 large tomato, peeled and chopped
Pinch of sugar
Salt and pepper

Place bacon at bottom of saucepan; add all other ingredients. Cover tightly and simmer for 10 to 15 minutes. Shake saucepan while cooking to mix ingredients. Serves 4.

NOPALES

(Cactus Leaves)

Most Mexican stores have *nopales,* the pulpy leaves of the nopal cactus. It comes in cans or jars, diced. Because the juice is viscous, like okra, I always drain and rinse the *nopales* in cold water. Personally, I could live without this vegetable, but you may like it. To me it has little flavor, but some people think it tastes rather like green pepper, though a little tart. I will admit that the crunchy texture is nice. Anyway, *nopales* are particularly relished when combined with wilted onion and red chile sauce and simmered, uncovered, until well saturated with sauce. This is good when used over fried pork chops. Another way is to wilt onion in oil, add the *nopales,* and heat well, then pour beaten eggs over them and scramble. Of course, I add salt and pepper to taste. If you use the fresh cactus leaves, handle them with care. Use tongs for holding them and cut off every needle, then peel and dice, and proceed as above, cooking a little longer than you do the canned kind.

COLACHE

(Mexican Succotash)

This Mexican version of succotash was probably learned from the Indians, as was the New England variety.

1 pound zucchini	*¼ cup butter*
4 ears corn	*1 small chopped onion*
1 pound tomatoes	*Salt and pepper*

Cut zucchini in small pieces, cut kernels from corn, peel and cube tomatoes. Cook onion in butter until lightly colored, add vegetables, salt and pepper, cover and simmer about 35 minutes or until vegetables are tender. Shake pan occasionally to prevent scorching. Serves 6.

CHILES RELLENOS CON QUESO

(Chiles Stuffed with Cheese)

This is an all-time favorite with Mexicans and Americans alike. Although *chiles rellenos* means stuffed chiles, it is usually assumed that they are cheese-stuffed. However, to be sure, order *chiles rellenos con queso,* when in a restaurant. This version, which is mine, is lighter and fluffier than the Mexican kind, but I find it's preferred by Americans. The stuffed chiles are reheated in a sauce, but I find that some of my friends prefer them plain, so suit yourself. This recipe makes 8 *chiles rellenos.*

¼ *pound Monterey Jack* *cheese*	2 *eggs*
1 *can peeled green chiles*	2 *tablespoons flour*
Flour	*Fat for frying*

Cut cheese in rectangles about ½ inch thick and 1 inch long. Wrap a strip of chile around each piece of cheese (each medium-sized chile makes two strips). Roll in flour. Make a batter by beating the whites of eggs until stiff and beating the yolks lightly. Fold yolks into whites, then fold in flour. Drop the stuffed and floured chiles into the batter one at a time. Pick up each with a spoon and transfer to a saucer; then slide from saucer into about 1½ inches of moderately hot oil in your frying pan. This keeps the chiles neater and holds more of the batter. Baste with hot oil or they may turn turtle. Fry until golden brown on each side, but work quickly! Drain them well on absorbent paper and let stand. Don't worry if the nice puffy coating deflates. It will puff up again when heated in this thin sauce before serving.

Sauce:

½ *medium-sized onion,*   *1 cup canned tomatoes*
   chopped   *2 cups chicken broth*
1 small clove garlic, crushed   *Salt, pepper, orégano*
1 tablespoon oil

Cook onion and garlic until wilted, in oil. Add tomatoes and press through a strainer. Put in a pot with the stock and bring to a boil, then season to taste with salt, pepper, and orégano rubbed between the palms of the hands. At serving time, heat the chiles in the boiling sauce for about 5 minutes. If frozen, cover and put in the oven for a few minutes (about 10 minutes) before putting in sauce. Chiles may also be stuffed with any meat, chicken or fish, or with picadillo. (See page 88).

CHILES RELLENOS CON QUESO
HECHOS MUY PRONTO

(Quick Chiles Stuffed with Cheese)

Here is a lazy way to do *chiles rellenos con queso*. It really tastes just as good but doesn't look as pretty.

Wrap the cheese with chiles and make the batter as in recipe for *Chiles Rellenos con Queso* (page 189). Put a tablespoon or two of oil in a large skillet, heat and pour in the batter, allow to coat a few seconds, then place the chile-wrapped cheese on half the batter. When the egg has set, fold the other half over the chiles, slide onto a hot platter and serve with or without the sauce.

SUGGESTIONS FOR USING CHILES POBLANOS

Chiles poblanos are what we get in cans, labeled peeled green chiles. They are indispensable in Mexican cookery.

Fill chiles with corn niblets, mixed with little pieces of Monterey Jack cheese and a little chopped pimiento. Mix cream with egg yolks and salt, pour over chiles, dot with pieces of cheese and bake at 325°F. until warmed through and cheese melts.

Fill chiles with picadillo (page 88), dip in egg batter as for chiles rellenos (page 189), and fry in hot oil. These do not require a sauce and can be served hot or cold.

Marinate chiles in oil, wine vinegar, or lemon juice and salt, for several hours. Drain and fill with sardines, shredded and mixed with a little peeled and chopped tomato, minced dry or green onion, a little orégano, and some of the dressing chiles were marinated in. Serve sprinkled with grated cheese. Tuna fish or shrimp may be used in place of sardines.

Marinate chiles in oil, wine vinegar, and salt for several hours. Fill with chopped leftover meats or chicken combined with chopped almonds and raisins. Spread the following mixture on top of them: Combine mashed avocado with cooked and mashed zucchini, add some of the dressing chiles were marinated in and salt. Don't worry about this turning black if it stands a while as the avocado stays green for a long time.

HOMINY AND BACON

I don't know how to translate hominy, but I am not going to leave this recipe out for that reason. It's too good.

4 strips bacon, cut in small pieces
3 cups hominy, drained

1½ cups milk
Salt and pepper

Fry bacon until crisp. Add hominy, milk, salt, and pepper. Cook over medium flame, stirring occasionally, until milk is completely absorbed. Makes 6 servings.

Ensaladas

❦ (Salads)

In Mexico salads are not served as often as they are in this country. They are usually what we would call a combination salad, using a mixture of vegetables with lettuce. This is almost always served with the main course. The Spanish are very fond of mixed green salads so they, too, are often served in Mexico. The typical salad dressing is quite tart—two parts olive or salad oil to one of wine vinegar, lime or lemon juice.

ENSALADA DE PAPAYA CON AGUACATE

(Papaya and Avocado Salad)

1 head of lettuce or romaine	½ cup olive oil
1 ripe papaya	1 teaspoon salt
2 avocados	Pepper
¼ cup of lime juice	

Arrange lettuce or romaine on six salad plates. Peel and slice papaya and avocados and put on lettuce, alternating the fruits. Combine remaining ingredients and serve as dressing. Serves 6.

ENSALADA DE NOCHE BUENA

(Christmas Eve Salad)

This salad, as its name suggests, is a holiday dish served always on Christmas Eve. In Mexico they include jicama, a fruit that I consider rather tasteless. I have left it out for that reason and because it's almost impossible to find in this country. I also serve mayonnaise with my version, but the Mexicans use sugar only.

2 *beets, cooked and sliced*
1 *cup pineapple cubes, fresh, canned, or frozen*
2 *apples, cored and sliced*
2 *oranges, peeled and sectioned*
1 *banana, sliced*
⅓ *cup raw peanuts*
Seeds from 1 pomegranate
Mayonnaise, thinned with cream

Arrange fruits attractively in a large glass bowl, sprinkling the pomegranate seeds and the peanuts on top. Pass the dressing separately. If you wish, you may add shredded lettuce to the fruit. I don't use the lettuce because it wilts if it's left over, but the rest of the salad is good the next day. Serves 6.

SALAD SUGGESTIONS

Marinate canned pimientos in oil, wine vinegar, and salt for 1 hour. When ready to serve, add sour cream and toss lightly.

Peeled tomatoes, stuffed with guacamole (page 8).

Marinate cold, cooked beef in olive oil, wine vinegar, salt and
pepper, for a couple of hours; then toss into bowl with lettuce,
tomatoes, onion rings, and green pepper rings.

Marinate oranges, peeled and thinly sliced, and thin slices of
onion in oil, wine vinegar, and salt for 30 minutes. Serve on crisp
lettuce, sprinkle with powdered chile tepin to taste.

ENSALADA DE COLIFLOR A LA ESPAÑOLA

(Cauliflower Salad, Spanish Style)

½ cup ripe olives
2 cups thinly sliced raw
   cauliflower (about ½
   small head)
⅓ cup finely chopped green
   pepper

¼ cup chopped pimiento
3 tablespoons chopped onion
Oil and wine vinegar
   dressing
Crisp lettuce leaves

Cut olives into small wedges. Combine with cauliflower, green
pepper, pimiento, onion, and salt to taste. Mix lightly with oil
and wine vinegar dressing. Refrigerate for several hours. When
ready to serve, toss gently to combine, then spoon into a nest
made of crisp lettuce leaves. Makes about 6 servings.

ENSALADA DE CAMARÓN CON HUEVO COCIDO

(Shrimp Salad with Hard-Cooked Eggs)

6 hard-cooked eggs, shelled
2 cups cooked or canned
   shrimp
2 cooked potatoes
3 tablespoons wine vinegar

¼ cup mayonnaise
¼ cup sour cream
½ teaspoon chile powder
Salt to taste

Chop 2 eggs coarsely, cube potatoes, and mix with shrimp. Combine these ingredients with 2 tablespoons vinegar and chill for several hours. When ready to serve, blend mayonnaise, sour cream, salt to taste, chile powder, and remaining tablespoon vinegar and combine with shrimp mixture. Turn into lettuce-lined salad bowl. Cut remaining eggs in quarters; arrange over salad. Makes 6 servings.

ENTREMES SURTIDO

(Appetizer Salad)

2 (15 oz.) cans asparagus tips
1 can pimientos
6 hard-cooked eggs, quartered

Onion rings, marinated in wine vinegar or pickled pearl onions

Dressing:

2 hard-cooked eggs, chopped
2 tablespoons capers
2 tablespoons chopped parsley
2 tablespoons chopped onion
2 tablespoons chopped green olives

½ cup olive oil
¼ cup wine vinegar
1 tablespoon prepared mustard
Salt and pepper

Arrange asparagus in center of large platter, pimientos, cut in half, at each end and eggs on each side of platter. Mix thoroughly all dressing ingredients, then pour over vegetables. Garnish with onions.

ALCACHOFAS EN SALSA DE MOSTAZA

(Artichokes in Mustard Sauce)

This is a favorite of one of my favorites, Emily Chase Leistner.

¼ cup wine vinegar
3 tablespoons oil
2 teaspoons horseradish
1 teaspoon salt
1 teaspoon Worcestershire
    sauce

1 clove garlic, mashed or
    pressed
2 tablespoons prepared
    mustard
12 to 18 cooked baby
    artichokes*

Combine all ingredients except artichokes; mix thoroughly. Marinate artichokes in this sauce for several hours before serving. Makes 1 cup sauce.

* Cook artichokes with a piece of lemon, clove of garlic, and salt to taste. If you can't get baby ones, use the frozen artichoke hearts, now available, and cook the same way.

ENSALADA DE FRIJOL

(Bean Salad)

3 tablespoons lemon juice
1 tablespoon wine vinegar
¼ cup olive oil
1 tablespoon minced onion
1 tablespoon minced parsley
1½ tablespoons chopped bell
    pepper

1 cup chopped celery
Pinch of thyme
¼ teaspoon orégano
Salt
1 (No. 303) can kidney
    beans, drained

Add all ingredients to the beans and marinate for about 2 hours before serving. Serves 4.

APERITIVO DE CAMARÓN A LA MEXICANA

(Mexican Shrimp Appetizer Salad)

This is a delicious salad. *But* you have to be very cautious in the amount of chile you use, or you will be angry with me. Chiles Jalapeños are hot, hot. This is served in Mexico as a first course.

½ *pound fresh shrimp, cooked and shelled*
⅓ *cup oil*
Juice of 2 lemons
Vinegar from chiles Jalapeños en escabeche
1 *small onion, minced*
2 *medium-sized tomatoes, peeled and chopped*

1 *small jar stuffed green olives*
2 *tablespoons minced parsley*
½ *teaspoon orégano, rubbed between palms of hands*
Salt to taste
1 *large avocado, cut in cubes*
Chiles Jalapeños

Marinate shrimp for 2 hours in oil, lemon juice, vinegar, and onion. Then add tomatoes, olives, parsley, orégano and salt. Mix well, and allow to stand 2 hours longer. When ready to serve, add avocado, and place in bowl lined with fresh lettuce. Garnish with strips of chiles Jalapeños. Serves 4.

PIMIENTOS MORRONES A LA LUPITA

(Lupita's Stuffed Pimientos)

Lupe Luna, a girlhood friend, gave me this recipe. I like it as much as I like her. The pimientos may be filled with tuna, salmon, shrimp, crab, chicken or cold meats, chopped, in place of sardines. They, too, are nice as a first course.

2 cans whole pimientos
2 tablespoons lemon juice
1 (3¾ oz.) can sardines in oil
2 hard-cooked eggs, chopped

1 tablespoon minced onion,
   dry or green
Crisp greens, with wine
   vinegar, oil and salt added
Grated Parmesan cheese

Turn pimientos and their liquid into small bowl; add lemon juice and marinate for several hours. Shred sardines; combine with eggs, onion, and oil from sardines; mix well. Drain pimientos, stuff with sardine mixture and arrange on platter over mixed greens. Pour liquid in which pimientos were marinated over all. Sprinkle with Parmesan and garnish with wedges of avocado. This is a beautiful salad! Serves 4 to 6.

ENSALADA DE COLIFLOR Y BETABELES

(Cauliflower and Beet Salad)

This is as good to eat as it is to look at. The beets give the cauliflower a lovely pink color.

1 medium-sized cauliflower,
   cooked (do not over-
   cook)
1 (8 oz.) can sliced beets
2 green onions, finely
   chopped

½ teaspoon orégano, rubbed
   between the palms of hands
Olive oil, wine vinegar, salt and
   pepper
Grated Parmesan cheese
   (optional)

Separate cauliflower into flowerettes and place in a bowl. Drain beets, cut slices in half and add to cauliflower. Add green onions. Make a dressing with the oil, vinegar, orégano, salt, and pepper and pour over vegetables. Toss lightly, turn onto a platter and serve, sprinkled with cheese. Serves 4 to 6.

ENSALADA DE GARBANZO

(Garbanzo Salad)

Here is another salad that is good to start the meal with. It's also wonderful when you want a hearty salad with charcoal-broiled meats.

1 *(14 oz.) can garbanzos,*   1 *tablespoon chopped parsley*
    drained   1 *small jar pimientos, chopped*
2 *tablespoons olive oil*   3 *green onions, chopped*
2 *tablespoons wine vinegar*   *Salt and pepper to taste*

Rinse garbanzos in cold water. Combine with other ingredients and allow to stand for several hours before serving. Serves 3 to 4.

ENSALADA ESMERALDA

(Emerald Salad)

A generous serving of this salad, some garlic French bread or Mexican rolls, and a dessert make a delightful luncheon. It is exceptionally good and lives up to its name, as it is a pretty shade of green.

1 *pound zucchini, cooked (do*   2 *peeled green chiles, cut in*
    not overcook)   *strips*
1 *(3 oz.) package cream*   *Oil, vinegar, salt, and pepper*
    cheese   *Romaine lettuce, chopped*
2 *tablespoons chopped onion*   *Pimiento-stuffed olives*
1 *avocado, cubed*

Cut zucchini in thick slices. Break cheese in pieces. Combine with onion, avocado, and chiles. Add oil, vinegar, salt, and pepper. Refrigerate for 20 to 25 minutes. Serve on bed of lettuce and garnish with olives. Serves 4 to 6.

Postres

&&

(Desserts)

The Mexicans always serve some little sweet at the end of a meal, even if it is only *cajeta de membrillo* (page 227) cookies, or sweet *empanadas*. They are very fond of milk desserts, *Flan* perhaps being their most famous.

PASTELITOS DE BODA

(Mexican Wedding Cakes)

My sister, Teresa Friend, a wonderful homemaker, always has some of these in her cooky jar.

¾ cup butter
4 tablespoons powdered
   sugar
2 teaspoons vanilla
1 teaspoon cold water

2 cups sifted all-purpose flour
⅛ teaspoon salt
1 cup finely chopped pecans
   or walnuts
Powdered sugar

Cream butter until fluffy, then add sugar, vanilla, and cold water. Mix thoroughly and stir in flour, salt, and nuts. Shape into a roll about 1½ inches in diameter. Wrap in waxed paper and chill thoroughly. Cut in ¼-inch slices and place on ungreased cooky sheet. Bake in a 400°F. oven for about 6 to 8 minutes, or until lightly browned. Remove from baking sheet and roll in powdered sugar while still hot. Place on rack to cool. Roll again in powdered sugar if desired. Makes 3½ to 4 dozen cookies. (These cakes may be made into small balls also, and baked for about 8 to 10 minutes. They should be rolled in sugar the same as the others.)

POLVORONES DE CANELA

(Mexican Cinnamon Tea Cakes)

1 cup butter	¼ teaspoon salt
½ cup confectioners' sugar	1 teaspoon vanilla
2¼ cups sifted all-purpose flour	2 cups confectioners' sugar, and 1 teaspoon
½ teaspoon cinnamon	cinnamon, for rolling

Cream butter and add sugar, flour, cinnamon, salt, and vanilla, making a moderately stiff dough. Chill in refrigerator for a few hours and then roll into small balls about 1 inch in diameter. Bake on a buttered cooky sheet in a 400°F. oven from 14 to 17 minutes. As soon as tea cakes are removed from oven, roll them in sugar and cinnamon mixture. Cool on a wire rack and then roll in sugar and cinnamon mixture again. Makes about 50.

SOPAIPILLAS

(Fried Bread)

These come from New, not Old Mexico. They are served as bread with butter, or with cinnamon and sugar.

1¾ cups sifted all-purpose flour
2 teaspoons baking powder

1 teaspoon salt
2 tablespoons shortening
⅔ cup cold water

Sift flour, baking powder, and salt into a mixing bowl; add shortening and cut in coarsely; then add cold water gradually. Mix just enough to hold together as for pie crust. Turn out on lightly-floured board and knead gently until smooth. Cover and let dough rest for five minutes; then roll out into a rectangle about 12 by 15 inches (dough should be very thin, about $\frac{1}{16}$- to ⅛-inch thick). Cut into 3-inch squares or 2- by 3-inch oblongs. Drop a few squares at a time into deep, very hot oil. At first, turn squares over 3 or 4 times to make them puff evenly. Fry about 2 or 3 minutes on each side, or until golden brown. The *sopaipillas* will puff up like little pillows. Serve hot as a bread with soup or guacamole. Makes about 20.

PLATÓN DE FRUTA FRESCA

(Fresh Fruit Platter)

Dear Esther Hall gave me this recipe. It's colorful and a delicious summer dessert.

1 (*No. 1 flat*) *can pineapple*
   slices
8 *watermelon fingers*
4 *slices of honeydew melon*

2 *bananas, cut diagonally*
12 *choice strawberries with*
   stems
Fresh mint

Chill pineapple in can. Drain well. Prepare melons. Clean strawberries, but leave stems on. Overlap slices of pineapple down center of large platter. Place watermelon fingers on either side. Fill in corners with honeydew slices and banana slices. Garnish with whole strawberries and mint leaves. Serve very cold. Yields 4 servings.

MANDARINAS EN JARABE DE COGNAC

(Tangerines in Cognac Syrup)

Select as many tangerines as desired, making sure to have them as uniform in size and appearance as possible. Place in a kettle and cover with water. When water comes to a boil, cook for 10 minutes. Drain off water and cool. Carefully prick bottom, top and sides of tangerines with a fork. To make the syrup, for each cup of water add ¾ cup of granulated sugar, a 2-inch stick of cinnamon, and 4 whole cloves. Add tangerines to syrup, making sure they are well covered. Bring to a boil, lower heat and simmer for 20 minutes. Push the tangerines down into the boiling syrup occasionally. Remove from heat and allow to cool in the syrup.

Add cognac to taste. These can be served as a dessert or as a garnish. If used as a garnish, make a stem and leaf by placing a mint leaf and a whole clove at the top of tangerines. They make a beautiful extra added attraction at a buffet dinner. These will keep very well for 3 or 4 days, if placed in a glass jar covered with the syrup and kept in the refrigerator.

DULCES DE CIRUELAS RELLENAS

(Mexican Prune Candy)

½ cup butter or margarine
1 cup brown sugar, packed
½ cup orange juice
2 cups sifted powdered sugar
1 tablespoon grated orange rind

1 cup chopped walnuts
1 teaspoon vanilla
4 dozen soft pitted prunes
(about 1 pound small prunes)

Melt butter in a heavy saucepan; add sugar and cook over low heat, stirring constantly, until sugar dissolves and mixture is bubbly. Add orange juice, boil vigorously until mixture forms a soft ball in cold water—234°F. on your candy thermometer—about 5 minutes. Remove from heat, cool without stirring, to luke-warm. Add powdered sugar, beat until creamy. Stir in orange rind, walnuts, and vanilla. Turn onto buttered platter, let stand until firm. Meanwhile, prepare prunes. If necessary, steam prunes a few minutes to soften them, or pour hot water over them, let stand 5 to 10 minutes and drain. Stuff candy into prunes. Makes 4 dozen small stuffed prunes.

FRESAS AZUCARADAS

(Candied Strawberries)

1 package strawberry-flavored
   gelatin
1 (7 oz.) package finely
   shredded coconut
2 tablespoons sweetened
   condensed milk
2 teaspoons vanilla

Red coloring—enough to
   obtain strawberry color
1 package strawberry gelatin
   (as is), for rolling
   strawberry cooky in after
   it is shaped

Mix all ingredients, except last, together thoroughly and form into strawberry shapes. Now roll in the dry gelatin and chill. To make green leaves and stems, use a butter-base frosting tinted green and apply with a pastry bag. Keep under refrigeration until ready to use. The strawberry cooky freezes well and so may be made in large amounts and stored in freezer. Makes about 2½ dozen cookies.

NOTE: These cookies are a wonderful decoration or garnish for cakes, frozen desserts, or fruit salads.

SUGGESTIONS FOR DESSERTS

Make a regular egg omelet, but sweeten it with sugar. Pour Kirsch over fresh, cleaned strawberries and allow to stand a few minutes. Cover omelet with strawberry-Kirsch mixture and sprinkle with powdered sugar.

Make a regular egg omelet, sweeten it and cut one ripe banana into it, before cooking. Garnish with sweetened whipped cream to which rum has been added.

Into a 10-inch spring form pan put scoops of lime and raspberry or strawberry sherbet. Make sure to alternate colors and do not crowd scoops. Cover it with softened (almost liquid) vanilla ice cream. Wrap top securely with aluminum foil and store in freezer immediately. When ready to use, remove side of spring pan and cut in wedges to serve. If you should use it at a birthday party, it is fancier covered with whipped cream and garnished with fruit, candies, nonpareils, or crushed peppermint sticks, to name a few.

FLAN #1

(Caramel Coated Custard—Basic Recipe)

This is a very popular dessert in Mexico and all my American friends like it.

1¾ cups sugar	2 teaspoons vanilla extract
8 whole eggs	6 tablespoons brandy or rum,
2 tall cans evaporated milk	warmed

Put 1 cup sugar into a deep pan in which the custard is to be baked and place over the heat, stirring constantly until the sugar melts and turns golden. Tip the pan around until it is entirely coated with the caramel; cool while making the custard. Beat eggs, add milk, remaining sugar, and vanilla. Mix well. Strain into the caramel-coated pan, cover and place pan in a larger pan containing hot water. (In Spanish this is called *"Baño de Maria,"* which means "Mary's Bath.") Bake custard at 350°F. for about 1 hour, or until a knife inserted in the center comes out clean. When ready to serve turn out on platter, pour brandy or rum over the flan, light, and send to the table flaming. Flans are at their best when made several hours before serving and thoroughly chilled. Serves 8 to 10.

Variations:

Orange Flan: Make as above, substituting orange juice for the milk, 1 teaspoon grated orange rind for the vanilla, and adding 2 more egg yolks. This will require an additional 15 or 20 minutes baking.

Coconut Flan: To basic recipe, add ½ cup grated coconut.

Almond Flan: Add ¼ pound blanched, ground almonds, to basic recipe.

Pineapple Flan: Use basic recipe, adding 1 flat can of crushed pineapple, well drained, at the bottom of pan before the sugar is completely cooled. This will take longer to cook than Basic Flan.

Banana Flan: To basic recipe, add 2 blended bananas.

Chocolate Flan: Add two or more tablespoons cocoa to basic recipe. Flans freeze very well.

FLAN #2

1 (15 oz.) can sweetened condensed milk	*4 eggs*
1 cup water	*1 teaspoon flavoring*
	Sugar for caramelizing

Beat eggs, add condensed milk, water, and flavoring. Follow the same procedure as for Flan #1 (page 207). Serves 6.

Variations:

Strong coffee may be added as part of the liquid.

Grated fresh or canned coconut may be added. If fresh is used, the coconut milk should be part of the liquid.

Add ½ cup ground pine nuts, pecans, or pistachio nuts to basic recipe.

Vegetable coloring could also be added to Flan to fit into a color scheme, if you want it.

NATILLA

(Caramel Custard)

My husband, Lawrence, christened our friend Essie Elliott "Santita"—that means "little saint." She loves this recipe. My mother used to caramelize the sugar by pressing it lightly with an old-fashioned flat iron, red hot.

3 cups milk	¼ teaspoon salt
6 egg yolks	1 teaspoon vanilla
1 cup milk	Additional sugar for
1 cup sugar	caramelizing
½ cup sifted flour	

Heat 2 cups of milk in top of double boiler until scalded. Thoroughly beat egg yolks with other cup of milk and add to scalded milk along with sugar, flour, and salt. Mix well and continue cooking over boiling water until thick and smooth, stirring constantly. Remove from heat. Let stand a few minutes, then add vanilla. Pour custard onto a large platter or into a shallow glass baking dish. When custard is entirely cold, sprinkle sugar generously over the top. Then place the platter or baking dish beneath the broiler until the sugar caramelizes all over the top. Let stand in the refrigerator for several hours before serving so that the caramelized sugar forms a sauce on top of the custard. Serves 6.

COCADA

(Coconut Pudding)

This the Mexicans go for, and so will you.

1 cup sugar	*1 quart milk*
1 cup water	*3 egg yolks, well beaten*
2 large cinnamon sticks	*¼ cup cold milk*
1 (3½ oz.) package shredded	
coconut	

Boil sugar, water, and stick cinnamon together for 10 minutes. Remove cinnamon, add coconut, and cook until coconut absorbs all of the syrup and is dry. Bring the quart of milk to a boil over low heat in deep saucepan; add coconut and cook mixture until of custard consistency, stirring frequently to prevent sticking. Mix eggs with cold milk, add to pudding and continue cooking slowly, stirring constantly until thick. Pour onto a buttered platter and allow to cool before refrigerating. This may be decorated with toasted almonds. Serves 6 to 8.

SUSPIROS DE MONJA

(Nun's Sighs)

My loyal, wonderful Dorothy Canet and I really had a workout
getting this recipe just right for you. Trouble to make? Yes, but if
you like sweets, don't miss these.

¼ cup butter or margarine
⅓ cup sugar
½ teaspoon salt
1 teaspoon grated lemon rind
½ cup water

1¾ cups sifted all-purpose
  flour
2 large eggs (or 3 medium
  size), slightly beaten
Powdered sugar for rolling

Into medium-size saucepan measure butter, sugar, salt, lemon
rind, and water. Bring quickly to a boil and immediately add, all
at once, flour. Beat rapidly with a spoon until mixture forms a
smooth ball and leaves sides of pan. Remove from heat and let
stand until lukewarm. Add eggs, stir until blended, then beat
vigorously until mixture forms a smooth, velvety thick paste. Chill
dough until easy to handle. Using small amounts of dough at a
time, turn out on well-floured board and pat or roll out to about
⅛-inch thickness. (Handle gently as dough will be fairly soft.)
Cut dough into 2- or 2½-inch squares. Lift with a spatula to
avoid stretching and drop squares into hot, deep fat, 350°F. Fry
until a rich golden brown on one side, about 2 minutes, then turn
and fry until browned on other side. Remove from fat, drain on
absorbent paper, and roll in powdered sugar. Makes about 2½
dozen.

ROSCA DE REYES

(King's Bread Ring)

King's Bread is served on Twelfth Night. The lucky (?) ones who get the dolls in their piece welcome the king and queen and must give a party on February 2nd, which is El Dia de la Candelaria (The Day of the Candle Mass).

2 cakes or packages of yeast	*3 eggs, well beaten*
2 tablespoons lukewarm	*⅓ cup soft shortening*
water	*4 cups sifted all-purpose flour*
⅔ cup boiling hot milk	*2 cups coarsely-grated or*
⅓ cup sugar	*finely-chopped candied*
1½ teaspoons salt	*fruits and citron*

Soften yeast in water. Combine hot milk, sugar, and salt, stirring to blend. Cool to lukewarm. Add softened yeast, well-beaten eggs, soft shortening, and half the flour. Beat until well blended. Add remaining flour and peels. Mix to moderately stiff dough. Knead lightly on floured board to smooth out dough. Shape* and place in greased pans or on baking sheet. Brush with melted shortening. Let rise in slightly warm place until double in bulk, about 1 hour and 10 minutes. Bake in a moderately hot oven, 375°F., for 25 to 30 minutes, or until bread is baked and nicely browned. Cool before slicing. Makes 1 large or 2 small rings.

To decorate: Spread cooled loaf with icing made by blending powdered sugar with milk or water to thick spread consistency. Spread over loaf and decorate with bits of candied fruit or peels.

* To shape dough: To make small rings, divide dough in half. Roll each half into a rope about 20-inches long, shape dough into 7- or 8-inch circles on greased baking sheet. (Or use ring molds.) Tuck two tiny china dolls into dough so that they won't show.

DULCE DEL SUR

(Southern Sweet)

⅓ cup butter or margarine
½ cup sifted powdered sugar
½ teaspoon cinnamon
Grated rind of one lemon
2 eggs
⅓ cup uncooked yellow corn meal
½ cup sifted all-purpose flour

1 teaspoon baking powder
¼ teaspoon salt
2 tablespoons currants, or chopped raisins
2 tablespoons pine nuts or chopped pecans
¼ cup cream

Sauce:

1 egg
⅓ cup sugar
1 teaspoon cornstarch

1 cup milk
2 tablespoons sherry

Cream butter, sugar, cinnamon, and lemon rind; beat in eggs. Sift corn meal, flour, baking powder, and salt directly into cream mixture; add raisins, nuts, and cream. Mix to a smooth batter and spoon into 6 buttered custard cups. Bake in a 350°F. oven for 20 minutes, or until done. Turn out in serving dishes and serve warm with the following sauce: Beat egg, sugar, cornstarch and milk until well blended. Cook slowly, stirring constantly, until slightly thickened, about 5 to 10 minutes, then add sherry. Serves 6.

BUDIN DE CHOCOLATE A LA ESPAÑOLA

(Chocolate Pudding, Spanish Style)

This Mexican pudding is unlike the common run of puddings.

¼ cup soft butter, margarine,
    or lard
¾ cup sugar
1 teaspoon vanilla
1 large egg
3 (1 oz.) squares
    unsweetened   chocolate,
    melted

1 ¾ cups sifted all-purpose
    flour
3 teaspoons baking powder
1 teaspoon salt
1 cup milk

Sherry sauce:

2 egg yolks
½ cup sugar

2 tablespoons sherry
1 ½ cups milk

Cream together until fluffy butter, sugar, and vanilla; add egg and chocolate; beat until well blended. Sift together flour, baking powder, and salt. Add to chocolate mixture alternately with milk. Mix to a smooth batter. Fill well buttered 2-quart pudding mold ⅔ full and cover tightly. Place mold on a rack in a large kettle of boiling water (water should come halfway up the mold). Steam pudding in continuously boiling water for 2 hours. Unmold and serve hot with sherry sauce: Beat egg yolks and sugar until well blended then beat in milk. Cook directly over moderate heat until slightly thickened, about 5 to 10 minutes, stirring constantly. Remove from heat and add sherry. Serve warm over *Budin de Chocolate.*

BUDIN DE MAIZ

(Corn Pudding)

Here's a corn pudding that isn't a corn pudding, but a dessert.
Your guests will come back for seconds.

3 ears large kernel corn
4 tablespoons sugar, or more if
   desired
1 teaspoon cinnamon

¼ teaspoon salt
3 tablespoons melted butter
2 eggs, separated

Break skin of corn kernels by grating it slightly, then scrape
with a table knife to remove all the pulp from the cob. By doing
this, you get all the pulp from the corn but the tough skins of
each kernel remain on the cob, giving the pudding a smoother
texture. Place all the corn pulp in a bowl; add sugar, cinnamon,
and salt. Beat the egg yolks slightly and add with butter to corn
mixture; mix well. Beat egg whites until fluffy, but not too stiff or
dry, and fold into corn mixture. Pour into a 1-quart casserole and
bake in a pan of water at 325°F. for about 1 hour and 15 minutes,
or until firm. The success of this recipe depends on the corn being
well matured. Serves 4 to 6.

PAN DULCE

(Sweet Bread)

For *desayuno,* in other words breakfast, with *café con leche* or chocolate. Good for *merienda,* too!

1 cake or package of yeast
½ cup lukewarm water
1 tablespoon sugar
1 teaspoon salt

3½ cups sifted all-purpose
*   flour*
2 tablespoons shortening
½ cup sugar
2 eggs, beaten

Topping:

½ cup sugar
¼ cup shortening
¼ teaspoon salt
1 teaspoon cinnamon

1 egg yolk
⅔ cup sifted all-purpose
*   flour*

Stir together yeast, water, sugar, and salt until yeast is softened. Add half of flour and beat well. Cover and let stand in slightly warm place until double in bulk—about 45 to 50 minutes. Cream shortening and sugar, then add eggs. Add to risen dough along with the remaining flour, beating well. Dough will be moderately soft. Cover and let rise again until double in bulk—about 1 hour. Turn out on floured board. Divide dough into 12 equal-size pieces and form each piece into a round flat bun, about 4-inches in diameter. Place buns on greased baking sheet. To make topping: Cream sugar, shortening, salt, and cinnamon until well blended. Add egg yolk, then flour, and stir until a crumbly mixture is formed. Spread topping on each bun. Cover and let rise until double—about 50 to 60 minutes. Bake in a 400°F. oven for about 15 minutes. Makes 12 buns.

ROSQUITAS PARA TÉ

(Little Wreaths for Tea)

Bridge players take note! These are especially good with a cup of Mexican chocolate about three o'clock in the afternoon.

¼ cup sugar

½ cup butter or margarine

1 teaspoon grated orange rind

3 egg yolks, beaten

2 cups sifted all-purpose flour

2 teaspoons baking powder

1 egg white, unbeaten

Measure sugar, butter, and orange rind into a mixing bowl. Cream together until light and fluffy. Add egg yolks. Mix until thoroughly combined. Then sift flour and baking powder together into mixture. Stir, forming a moderately stiff dough. Turn out on a lightly-floured board and roll ½-inch thick. Cut with a 2½-inch doughnut cutter. Place cookies on a lightly-greased baking sheet and brush with egg white. Bake in a 375°F. oven for 20 minutes, until lightly browned. Makes 8 large cookies, or 16 smaller ones.

CHURROS

(Mexican Crullers)

Churros are to the Spanish and Mexicans what doughnuts are to the Americans. And they are great served with chocolate or coffee. Sometimes they are made in one long spiral, forcing the dough into the deep fat all in one piece. These are quite spectacular.

1 slice bread
½ lemon
1 cup sifted all-purpose flour
1 teaspoon salt

1 cup boiling water
1 large egg, unbeaten
Oil for frying
Powdered sugar for rolling

Before preparing batter for *churros,* start heating in a large pan the oil in which they are to be fried. Add bread and lemon to the oil. When bread is very dark brown (almost burned) remove bread and lemon. You'll find this preliminary gives a distinctive flavor to the *churros* when they are fried. Sift flour and salt into a mixing bowl. Make a well in center of flour and add boiling water. Beat vigorously until fluffy and smooth. Add egg and continue beating until batter is smooth and shiny. Then pour into a paper cornucopia or pastry tube and drop small amounts (about 3 inches in length) into the very hot oil. When *churros* are golden brown all over, remove them to absorbent paper to drain. While still hot, roll each one in powdered sugar. Yields 1 dozen *churros.*

MOLLETES

(Sweet Rolls)

1 cup milk
1½ teaspoons anise seed
2 tablespoons lard or
    shortening
⅓ cup granulated sugar
1½ teaspoons salt

1 large egg, slightly beaten
1 cake moist compressed
    yeast
2 tablespoons warm water
4¼ cups sifted all-purpose
    flour

To milk in saucepan add anise seed and bring just to the boiling point. Remove from heat. Add shortening, sugar, and salt. Mix well and let cool to lukewarm. Add egg and yeast (softened in warm water). Stir until well blended and add flour. Mix well, making a soft dough. Cover with a damp cloth and let stand in warm place until double in bulk, about 1 hour. Turn out on floured board and divide dough into 24 equal-size pieces. Shape into balls and place 2 inches apart on a well greased baking sheet. Cover with damp cloth and let rise until double in bulk, about 50 minutes. Brush lightly with a little melted shortening. Bake in a 400°F. oven for 15 minutes. Yields 2 dozen medium-sized rolls.

TORTA TROPICAL

(Tropical Torte)

When I was discussing plans for this book with Myron Boardman, Vice-President of Prentice Hall, I served him Torta Tropical. He liked it so much he said he hoped I would include it in the book. And I took him at his word.

6 egg whites	⅓ cup pine nuts
½ teaspoon cream of tartar	¼ cup candied cherries, cut in
¼ teaspoon salt	small pieces
1½ cups sugar	1 cup cream, whipped
1 teaspoon vanilla extract	

Preheat oven to 400°F. Beat egg whites until foamy; add cream of tartar and salt. Continue beating until egg whites stand in soft peaks. Add sugar gradually and keep on beating until egg whites are very stiff. Add vanilla. Lightly fold in pine nuts and cherries. Butter an 8-inch spring form pan; pour in mixture and place in oven. Turn off heat immediately and leave torte for no less than 12 hours in oven. Be sure not to peek! Remove from oven and release from spring pan. Cover entire torte with whipped cream. Decorate by sprinkling over a few of the pine nuts and cherries.

This torte may be varied by using ½ cup finely-shredded coconut or ½ cup well-drained, crushed pineapple in place of the pine nuts and cherries. It can also be made plain and served with lightly sweetened crushed fresh fruits. Nice for summer months when fruits are varied and plentiful. Serves 8.

BUÑUELOS

(Mexican Fritters)

As a young girl in Mexico, I remember the *buñuelos* being shaped by placing a clean napkin over the knee and patting until the dough was flat and round. I'm sure there is a more modern method today. However, they will taste just the same and are a nice Christmas season sweet.

4 cups sifted all-purpose flour　　*2 eggs, beaten*
2 tablespoons sugar　　　　　　　*¾ cup milk, approximately*
1 teaspoon baking powder　　　　*¼ cup butter, melted*
2 teaspoons salt

Sift dry ingredients into a bowl; beat together eggs and milk and add to dry ingredients. Then add butter and mix into a dough that can be easily handled without being sticky. Add one or two more tablespoons of milk if necessary. Turn dough out on a lightly-floured board and knead until very smooth. Divide into 18 to 24 pieces, shape into balls, cover them with a cloth and let stand for 20 minutes. Roll each ball on a lightly-floured board into a large round, about the size of a large *tortilla*. Let the rounds stand 5 minutes, then fry in deep, hot oil until they are a light golden brown all over. As each one finishes frying, remove it to absorbent paper to drain. *Buñuelos* may be served sprinkled with cinnamon and sugar or with thin honey. A favorite way is to break them up into a large soup bowl and serve with a thin brown sugar syrup flavored with stick cinnamon. These freeze well. Wrap each separately in foil, because they are fragile. Crisp them in the oven before serving. Makes about 1½ to 2 dozen large *buñuelos*.

PAN DE FIESTA

(Festive Fruit Bread)

Gladys Wessel, one of my favorite friends, brought this recipe from Mexico.

½ cup hot milk	1 egg, beaten
¼ cup shortening	½ cup mixed candied fruit and
¼ cup sugar	peel, finely chopped
1½ teaspoons salt	¼ cup walnuts, chopped
1 cake or package of yeast	½ teaspoon cinnamon
½ cup water	3 cups sifted all-purpose flour

Stir together milk, shortening, sugar, and salt. Soften yeast in water. When milk mixture is cool, stir in yeast, egg, candied fruit, nuts, and cinnamon. Add flour, mixing to a moderately stiff dough (this dough will be slightly softer than regularly kneaded dough). Shape into a loaf and place in greased bread pan 10 × 5 × 3 inches. Cover and let rise in a warm place until double in bulk, about 1 to 1½ hours. Bake in a 375°F. oven for 35 to 40 minutes. Cool thoroughly before storing or slicing. Makes 1 loaf.

NOTE: Loaf may be glazed while still warm with a little powdered sugar mixed to spreading consistency with water, milk, orange juice or sherry.

TORTA BORRACHA

(Drunken Torte)

Dr. Berta Shelton, a girlhood friend, of Chihuahua, Mexico, gave me this inebriated dessert. This torte is a heavy drinker, *for sure*. You'll be surprised to see all the syrup disappear.

4 eggs, separated
½ cup sugar
1 cup flour
1 teaspoon baking powder

¼ teaspoon salt
1 teaspoon vanilla
⅓ cup melted butter

Beat whites of egg stiff with 4 tablespoons of the sugar. Beat the yolks with the rest of the sugar and add to the whites. Fold in dry ingredients and lastly add the melted butter and vanilla. Pour into a 2-quart casserole and bake at 375°F. for 30 minutes. When done make holes all over with an ice pick or skewer and pour the following sauce all over it.

Sauce:

2 cups sugar
2 cups water

½ cup brandy, rum, or sherry

Boil the water and sugar until it makes a soft ball, then add whatever liquor you are using. Pour on cake. Before liquid is all absorbed, sprinkle generously with finely chopped nuts or grated coconut. Serves 8.

NOTE: This cake can be served alone or with vanilla ice cream, as it resembles a Rum Baba.

PAN DE MUERTO

(Bread of the Dead)

This is served on the Day of the Dead, or All Saints' Day. In Mexico, this bread is decorated by shaping small "bones" from a portion of the dough and placing them on the loaf in the shape of a cross before baking. Wonderful with coffee or Mexican chocolate.

½ cup milk

¼ cup sugar

1 teaspoon salt

¼ cup shortening (part butter
    for flavor)

1 whole egg, plus 1 egg yolk,
    beaten

1 cake or package of yeast

2¾ cups sifted all-purpose
    flour

Bring milk to boiling. Remove from heat and stir in sugar, salt, and shortening. Add eggs and yeast and beat until mixture is well blended and yeast is dissolved. Add flour and mix to a moderately stiff dough. Turn out on a floured board and knead lightly a few minutes until dough is smooth. Cover with a damp cloth and let rest on the board 30 minutes. Cut dough into 3 equal-sized pieces and roll each piece into a rope 12-inches long. Make a braid of the three ropes, pressing ends together to seal them; then place braid on a lightly greased cookie sheet. Cover with damp cloth and let rise in a warm place until light and double in bulk, about 1½ hours. Brush with melted shortening and bake in a 375°F. oven for 25 to 30 minutes. If desired, brush baked loaf with melted butter after taking it from oven. Cool loaf thoroughly before slicing.

ROSCAS DE VINO BLANCO

(Ring Cookies with White Wine)

½ cup oil

  Peel from ½ lemon or
    orange

1 teaspoon anise seed

½ cup white table wine

2 cups sifted all-purpose flour

¼ cup sugar

½ teaspoon salt

½ teaspoon cinnamon

¼ cup sugar

½ teaspoon cinnamon

Place oil and peel in a saucepan over moderate heat. Heat until peel turns golden brown. Remove from heat and remove peel.

Add anise seed. Cool to room temperature. Add wine, flour, sugar, salt, and cinnamon. Beat until mixture forms a smooth ball, leaving sides of pan clean. Using a tablespoonful of dough for each cooky, roll between floured palms into a rope about 6-inches long. Place in a ring shape on an ungreased baking sheet, pinching ends of dough together to seal. Bake for about 20 minutes in a 375°F. oven. Roll hot cookies in mixture of sugar and cinnamon. Cool thoroughly before storing. Yields about 2 dozen cookies.

ROSCAS DE YEMAS
(Egg Yolk Rings)

3 egg yolks
¼ cup oil
¼ cup sugar
½ teaspoon salt

¼ teaspoon anise extract (or
½ teaspoon anise seed)
¾ to 1 cup sifted all-purpose
flour
Powdered sugar

Measure into a mixing bowl egg yolks, oil, sugar, salt, and anise extract. Beat until well blended and creamy. Add flour. Mix to a moderately stiff dough. Use a well-floured board and handle dough gently. (Dough is soft and stretches easily but is not sticky.) Take about one tablespoon dough at a time and roll, using palms of hands, to pencil length, about 7-inches. Place on lightly greased cooky sheet and shape into a ring. Bake in a 350°F. oven for 8 to 10 minutes. Remove from oven and roll in powdered sugar. Let cookies cool thoroughly before storing. Makes about 1½ dozen.

CUERNITOS

(Little Horns)

These are called little horns, because they are the shape of a bull's horns. Good, too, whether you are a matador or not.

2½ cups sifted all-purpose
    flour
1 teaspoon salt
¾ cup butter or margarine
2 egg yolks
2 to 3 tablespoons cold
    water

Thick jam or preserves
1 egg, beaten
⅓ cup finely-chopped
    blanched almonds
Powdered sugar for rolling

Measure flour, salt, and butter into a mixing bowl. Work butter into flour until finely divided, as for pie crust. Add egg yolks and water. Mix with a spoon or hands to form a stiff dough. Divide dough into 24 even-sized pieces and shape into balls. Roll each ball on floured board (or pat with floured fingers) into small rounds about 2½- to 3-inches in diameter. In center of each round, place a small amount of jam or preserves. Roll over to enclose jam and press edges together to prevent filling from running out. Place on ungreased baking sheets. Shape filled rolls into small horns or crescents. Brush each with beaten egg and sprinkle top with almonds. Bake 12 to 15 minutes in a 375°F. oven, or just until a light golden brown. Remove from baking sheet and roll carefully in powdered sugar. Cool before storing. Makes about 2 dozen.

NOTE: This is a very short, rich dough. Handle gently to prevent breaking or tearing so filling does not run out during baking.

GALLETAS ELENA

(Elena's Cookies)

While these cookies carry my name they are not really my own specialty, but are very popular in Mexico. There's more than one Elena in Mexico.

½ *cup soft butter*
⅔ *cup sugar*
3 *egg yolks*
1½ *cups sifted all-purpose flour*

½ *teaspoon baking powder*
½ *teaspoon salt*
1 *teaspoon vanilla*
¼ *cup nonpareils (tiny colored decorating candy)*

Cream butter, sugar, egg yolks, and vanilla together. Sift flour, baking powder, and salt into creamed mixture and stir, making a smooth dough. Shape dough into small balls. Poke your thumb in center of each ball making a hole. Shape into small rings. Dip each ring in tiny candies. Bake on lightly-greased cooky sheets in 375°F. oven until lightly browned—about 10 to 12 minutes. Cool before storing. Makes 2½ dozen rings.

DULCE DE LECHE Y PIÑA

(Mexican Pineapple Milk Pudding)

Mexicans like their desserts very sweet, as this recipe will indicate. It, or something very much like it, can be made by simmering an unopened can of sweetened, condensed milk in water to cover for 3 hours. Cool it, open both top and bottom of can, turn out and slice. If you want something extra special, put on top of a slice of pineapple, add a spoonful of whipped cream, and sprinkle with chopped almonds. There goes your diet!

1 cup sugar
6 egg yolks, well beaten
1 quart cold milk

½ cup blanched almonds,
   ground very fine
1 cup crushed pineapple,
   drained

Add sugar and beaten yolks to milk. Heat slowly, stirring constantly, until milk starts to boil. Add ground almonds and continue cooking and stirring until mixture thickens. Add drained pineapple and cook a few minutes longer. Pour into serving dish and sprinkle with a little powdered cinnamon. Serve very cold. Serves 6.

CAJETA DE MEMBRILLO

(Pressed Quince Paste)

You'll need a weather eye for this, because it has to stand in the sun for a couple of days. It's typically Mexican, as are mango and guava pastes, made in exactly the same way. I like to serve it for dessert, with Jack cheese, or at tea or *merienda* time.

Wash quinces and steam until tender—about 20 minutes. Cut in quarters, removing core and seeds. (I have learned it's much easier to core and seed after steaming.) Grind through the finest blade of your food chopper, skin and all. Measure out the quince pulp and add an equal amount of sugar. Mix well and place in a pot that is easy to hold on to, as you are going to do a lot of stirring. Use a wooden spoon and stir constantly, as the mixture cooks, or it will burn. When the mixture is quite thick and you can see the bottom of the pan clearly, empty it into a square or oblong pan and cool. When cold, the cooked quince is turned out on a waxpaper-covered board, covered with cheesecloth, and placed in the sun for 2 days. Turn the board around occasionally to expose all surfaces to the sun, as this treatment prevents molding. Store the pressed quince paste, covered, in a cool dry place.

CAPIROTADA

(Mexican Bread Pudding)

This dessert is usually served during Lent. The combination of cheese and fruits may sound strange, but it's extremely popular in Mexico and I know many Americans who rave over it.

1 quart water
1 pound brown sugar
3-inch stick cinnamon
1 whole clove
6 slices toast, cubed (or equivalent of leftover pound cake)

3 bananas or apples, sliced
1 cup raisins
1 cup peanuts, chopped
½ cup blanched almonds, chopped
½ pound Monterey Jack cheese, cubed

Boil water, sugar, stick cinnamon, and clove together until syrupy. Butter a casserole generously and put in a layer of bread or cake cubes. Cover with a layer of banana or apple slices and sprinkle with some of the raisins, peanuts, almonds, and cheese cubes. Repeat the layers until all ingredients are used. Remove stick cinnamon and clove from syrup and pour syrup over pudding. Bake in a 350°F. oven about 30 minutes. Serve hot. Serves 6.

FLAN DE CALABAZA

(Pumpkin Flan)

This recipe is from Helen Brown's *Holiday Cook Book*.

1⅔ cups sugar	1 teaspoon salt
3 cups thin cream	¼ cup Jamaica rum
2 cups strained pumpkin	6 eggs

Put a cup of granulated sugar into a round deep dish (such as Pyrex, enameled iron, earthenware, or other heat-proof oven dish) and allow it to melt over a low heat (better use an asbestos mat!) stirring constantly. When it is an even deep amber, remove from the heat and tip quickly in all directions so that the sides and the bottom of the dish will be coated. In the meantime, scald cream, add pumpkin, salt, remaining ⅔ cup of sugar, rum, and eggs, slightly beaten. Pour this mixture into the dish, place it in a pan of water, and bake at 350°F. for an hour, or until a knife inserted into the center comes out shining clean. Allow to cool, then invert on a round serving dish. The bottom will be a glorious shiny brown. This may be served chilled or warm, flaming with rum. Serves 6 to 8.

Frutas

꧁ (Fruits)

Mexicans, like Americans, love fruit, and they have some wonderful semitropical ones. Pineapples and guavas, mangoes, papayas, avocados, coconuts, chirimoyas, pomegranates, bananas, and zapotes are all grown in Mexico and are used lavishly. So, too, are oranges, lemons, and those wonderful Mexican limes that look like miniature oranges. Most of these fruits are eaten raw, though not always. Mangoes, a great favorite, are often stewed, but they are also sliced when ripe and eaten for *desayuno,* or dessert. They are delicious when used in making ice cream, and are fine in fruit cocktails. Pomegranate seeds often turn up in the most unexpected places, as a garnish for a salad, or to add color and interest to some meat or poultry dish, or in puddings, or sprinkled over ice cream, or in compotes—and, pomegranate juice is delicious! Guavas are eaten out of hand, or stewed, but the guava shells, available in cans, are also stuffed with *queso fresco* (I use cream cheese) and served as a dessert. Coconut goes into many desserts, candies, and cookies, and even into beverages, and is very popular. So is pineapple. Avocados are so plentiful that one spread, a kind of guacamole, is called *mantequilla de pobre,* or poor man's butter. Additionally, they are used as a garnish with many Mexican dishes, but are never cooked. Papayas, on the other hand, are good baked, though they are more often eaten raw. Mexico has melons, too, and most of the fruits that we have in this country; they are served in the same ways.

Brebajes

🍵 (Beverages)

Beverages in Mexico are almost as varied as they are in the United States. Coffee is popular and so, too, is Mexican chocolate. Soft drinks, including, of course, the now universal *Coca-Cola,* and the Mexican *sidra,* or cider, are well liked. Mexico also has several good wines of its own and its *cerveza,* or beer, is considered as good as any in the world. *Tequila,* the national alcoholic drink, is used in many mixed drinks, but the classic way to take it is with salt and lemon. Put a little salt on the back of your hand, lick it off, toss down a "shot" of *tequila,* then suck on a wedge of lemon. *Mescal,* a lower grade *tequila,* is used by the very poor. Mexico also has its own brandy, called *aguardiente,* and a drink called *pulque,* which is the lightly fermented juice of the cactus. Then there are the *atoles,* a sort of gruel, and *champurrado,* which is chocolate-flavored gruel.

CAFÉ CON LECHE

(Coffee with Milk)

This, like *café au lait,* is a favorite way of drinking coffee in Mexico. They make a very strong brew of coffee—really an essence —and dilute it to their taste with hot milk. I suppose by now they are using an instant coffee for this national drink, at least in the cities where it is available.

CHOCOLATE MEXICANO

(Mexican Chocolate)

Mexican chocolate may be bought at any Mexican store. It comes in rounds, marked off in quarters, and is sweetened. For each cup of heated milk, add one of these sections. When dissolved, pour into a jug, or pitcher (called a *jarro* in Mexico) in which it will be sent to the table. Then with a *molinillo* (a wooden mill which is twirled between the hands), beat vigorously until the chocolate foams. If you cannot get Mexican chocolate, use American sweet chocolate, but flavor it with a little cinnamon. Some Mexicans add an egg white to their chocolate to make it foam but this I never do. It isn't necessary if you use a little elbow grease when beating. The *molinillo* is so picturesque I prefer to use it, but an egg beater or a portable electric mixer does the job, I admit.

ATOLE DE ALMENDRA
(Almond Gruel)

Atole is a sort of gruel, variously flavored, always sweetened and enjoyed by children and adults alike. It is sometimes made with cornstarch. A similar drink, called *champurrado,* always contains chocolate.

½ cup masa	½ cup blanched ground
2 cups water	almonds
1 stick cinnamon	1 quart milk
1 cup sugar	3 egg yolks, beaten

Dissolve masa in water, add cinnamon and cook, stirring, over low heat, until slightly thickened. Add sugar, almonds, combined with some of the milk, and remaining milk. Continue cooking, stirring all the time. When it thickens, remove from heat, add egg yolks and cook just until it comes to a boil. Serve hot.

Variations:

Atole de piña: Add one can of crushed pineapple in place of almonds.

Atole de fresa: Add one basket of crushed strawberries in place of the almonds.

GARAPIÑA

1 large pineapple, peeled and
  ground
½ pineapple rind, finely
  chopped
½ cup tamarindos (available
  in Mexican stores),
  peeled and washed

Juice of 6 oranges
1 stick cinnamon
6 whole cloves
1 pound sugar
4½ quarts water

Combine all ingredients and mix well. Place in large crockery jar, cover, and keep in a cool place for 3 days. Strain and serve very cold.

PONCHE DE PIÑA

(Pineapple Punch)

½ cup sugar
1½ cups water
4 sticks cinnamon
12 cloves

1 (46 oz.) can pineapple
  juice
1½ cups of canned or fresh
  orange juice
½ cup lemon juice

This punch is unusual in flavor, but easy to make. Simmer sugar, water, cinnamon, and cloves for about 30 minutes. Strain and add pineapple, orange, and lemon juice. Pour over ice or frozen pineapple juice cubes. Makes about 2 quarts of punch.

I do not drink myself but I always serve something to my friends who do. Philip Brown knows a lot about mixing drinks—not that he's a *borracho,* it's just that he likes to play bartender. Many of these cocktail recipes are his.

VERACRUZ COCKTAIL

2 parts tequila, 1 part port wine. Stir with ice and lemon peel.

MARGARITA

3 parts tequila, 1 part Cointreau, juice of ½ lime. Pour over crushed ice, stir. Rub rim of stem glass with rind of lime and spin in salt. Strain cocktail into glass and sip through salt rim.

YUCATÁN

2 parts pineapple juice, 1 part green crême de menthe, 2 parts tequila. Shake well with crushed ice, strain into cocktail glass.

TEQUILA SOUR

2 jiggers tequila, 1 teaspoon sugar, juice of ½ lemon, dash of Pernod (or bitters). Shake hard with cracked ice. Pour into old-fashioned or whisky sour glass and add squirt of seltzer.

TEQUILA SUNRISE

1 jigger tequila, 2 dashes grenadine, ½ lime (juice and peel), 6 dashes crême de cassis. Place ingredients in tall stemmed glass with several ice cubes. Add squirt of seltzer or two and stir lightly.

TEQUILA DAISY

2 jiggers tequila, ½ jigger lemon juice, ½ jigger grenadine, 1 jigger charged water. Shake vigorously with ice, and strain into cocktail glasses. Sugar may be added if desired.

FELIPE MORENO'S COCTEL

(Philip Brown's Cocktail)

2 parts tequila, 1 part Kahlua. Stir with cracked ice, strain into cocktail glass and add twist of lemon peel.

TAXCO FIZZ

2 jiggers tequila, 1 teaspoon sugar, juice of 1 lime, 1 egg white, soda. Shake vigorously with cracked ice, strain into 8-ounce glass, fill with cold soda water.

ESPECIALIDAD DE LA CASA

(Specialty of the House)

My friends particularly like these two cocktails that I make for them. I like them, also, because I can make either up ahead of time and keep in a jar in the refrigerator until needed.

Combine equal parts of tequila and pineapple juice, add grenadine to color, chill, and pour over crushed ice in glasses.

COCTEL DE TEQUILA Y TORONJA

(Tequila and Grapefruit)

1 (No. 2) can grapefruit juice, 3 ounces grenadine, 2 ounces lemon juice, 1 teaspoon orange bitters, 3 cups tequila. Combine all ingredients and chill thoroughly before serving. Makes about 1½ quarts.

ROMPOPE

(Eggnog)

In Mexico, it is customary to offer friends a small glass of *Rompope* when they stop in for a visit in the late afternoon.

1 *quart milk*	¼ *cup ground almonds*
1 *cup sugar*	(*optional*)
1 *stick cinnamon or 1-inch*	12 *egg yolks, beaten*
vanilla bean	1 *cup brandy*

Combine milk, sugar, and cinnamon stick. Heat to boiling, stirring frequently. Reduce heat and continue cooking, stirring constantly for 10 minutes. Remove from heat and cool to lukewarm, stirring occasionally to prevent scum from forming. When cool, add almonds and beaten egg yolks. Return to heat and cook slowly until spoon is well coated and mixture is slightly thickened. Cool again, stirring frequently, until liquid falls to room temperature. Stir in brandy and store in refrigerator until ready to serve. Makes about 1½ quarts.

CARLOTTA'S DREAM

2 ounces tequila, juice of ½ lemon or lime, sugar, champagne. Put 4 ice cubes in a 10-ounce glass, add tequila, lemon juice, and sugar to taste; fill glass to top with champagne.

AZTEC PUNCH

1 gallon tequila
  Juice of 12 lemons
  Sugar to taste
1 gallon grapefruit juice

2 quarts strong tea (cold)
3 sticks cinnamon (or 1½
    teaspoons ground)

Pour over ice in punch bowl. Makes about 3 gallons.

FIESTA CHAMPAGNE PUNCH

Place 1 quart pineapple sherbet in a punch bowl. Add 1 large bottle champagne, well chilled. Stir well. Serve in champagne glasses or punch cups. (Orange, lemon, or raspberry sherbet may replace the pineapple with equally delicious results.) Makes about 20 (3 oz.) servings.

SANGRIA

Mix the juice from 4 lemons and 1 orange with ½ cup sugar. Strain, add one large (⅘ quart) bottle red table wine. Serve in tall glasses, half-filled with crushed ice. Makes 8 servings.

SANGRILLA

Here is Sangria's Spanish cousin—so close in basic ingredients and name it could be a kissing cousin.

Muddle fresh fruit, peaches, pears or oranges in a large, tall glass. Sweeten a bit, add red table wine and a squirt of seltzer.

KAHLUA AND COGNAC

This makes a delicious after-dinner drink. Half fill a liqueur glass with Kahlua. Then fill almost to the top with cognac. Float a spoonful of heavy cream on top. Serve after dinner, with coffee.

BERTA

This is the famous Taxco drink.

Put an ounce and a half of tequila in a tall glass, filled with ice, add the juice of a lime, one ounce of special syrup (see below) and fill glass with charged water.

Syrup:

4 cups water   *1 egg white, well beaten*
4 cups sugar

Cook sugar and water together until clear, cool, and add the egg white.

Entertaining in

❦ la casa de Elena

One of life's greatest pleasures is having friends in my home to break bread, or more appropriately tortillas, with me. Preparing for guests is not work. I honestly love every minute spent in the kitchen.

Because of my blindness, I have learned the importance of doing as much as possible well in advance. And more and more I realize this is necessary for every hostess, if she wants to be relaxed. The freezer is invaluable to my style of "beforehanded" cooking. And, thank fortune, Mexican and Spanish foods take kindly to freezing—even Flan.

As soon as a date is set, I get going at top speed. First, I plan a menu. Naturally I don't write mine on paper—just in my memory—but I think it would be smart for you to do so. With the menu in mind, I set a time schedule for preparing the various dishes. When the appointed dinner hour comes, I am all set—except for last minute details. After all, let's face it. I'm selfish and I like to enjoy my own parties as well as the next one.

And now to some ways of adapting my recipes to your home

entertaining. It seems to me you'll find that Mexican and Spanish foods and customs will add flair and flavor to your entertaining.

Let's begin with morning get-togethers. Next time you have a committee, club, or neighborhood coffee gathering, why not serve Mexican chocolate for a change? It's rich enough so that you may skip the ordinary sweet rolls. Or if calories aren't your problem (look who's talking) you could include *Pan Dulce* (page 216) or *Buñuelos* (page 220). If you want to give a real party, you could correctly invite your friends to a *Desayuno,* for that is what the first meal of the day is called in Mexico, as you probably learned in the preface.

Brunch, or *Almuerzo,* as the second breakfast is called in Mexico, is such a wonderful way to entertain on weekends. To give yours a Mexican fillip, follow me. Papaya, guava, or pineapple juice, or the fresh fruits themselves get the meal off to a nice start. Eggs are next, and you'll find a number of delicious ways to fix them in this book. It is customary in Mexico to serve steak with them. At the price of beef now, I'll let you decide about following this custom! You just must serve refried beans, in the good company of your favorite chile sauce, plenty of hot tortillas, and coffee, and believe me you've got a reputation as a "hostess with the mostess."

VAMOS AL CAMPO

(Let's Go Picnicking)

A picnic is as much of an adventure in Mexico as it is here. The preparations the day before, the getting up early in the morning to make use of all the sunshine possible—all this is a lot of fun. But the highlight of the picnic is the food. If it is good, the adventure is a success; if not, it's a big flop. I'm going to give you my idea of a successful *dia de campo* (picnic).

Let's start with a salad; *Ensalada Esmeralda* (page 200). This can be prepared ahead of time, but take the avocado along and add it when ready to serve. If you prefer, a tossed green salad could replace the above. Just take assorted greens in a plastic bag and your favorite dressing in a jar, and toss it at the last minute. You'll want radishes and olives, too, and romaine lettuce if you are taking the Emerald Salad.

Pierna De Carnero a la Mexicana (page 97) is ideal for picnics. Roast it the day before, slice, place on a platter, cover with waxpaper or a plastic wrap and it's ready to pick up the next morning. If you prefer chicken, I suggest *Pollo Encanelado* (page 256).

A Mexican picnic is not complete without *Chiles Rellenos,* these minus the sauce and either with cheese (page 189), with *Picadillo* or sardines (page 130). They can be prepared the day before as they are delicious served cold. For another treat I suggest *Tortas De Calabacitas* (page 184). Of course, the ever-popular beans in some form or another are also a "must."

Hot tortillas would be ideal, but this is not possible unless you have an outdoor grill and a skillet to heat them. Otherwise you'll have to be satisfied with French rolls cut in half and buttered, or *tostaditas.* If you desire, you may make *Tortitas Compuestas* (page 21) using French rolls.

Now comes the dessert, and as far as I'm concerned this makes any meal complete, for do I ever love desserts! I think *Cocada* (page 210) would be nice. So would *Dulces De Ciruelas Rellenas* (page 205), or assorted cookies (you'll find many recipes for them in the dessert category), or plenty of fresh fruit and cheese.

Lots of hot coffee or Mexican chocolate in a thermos will make a happy ending to our *dia de campo.*

TAMALADA

Tamales are strictly fiesta fare and the parties at which they are the number one food are called *Tamaladas.* You know tamales freeze so well, they can be made many days before the party and steamed before serving. Have plenty of refried beans for this party, too. The usual coffee, *Atole* (page 235) or *Champurrado* (page 235) would be agreeable company. For dessert in watermelon season, I think you'd like to serve a scrumptious looking dessert I dreamed up for *Good Housekeeping* magazine once. To prepare it, just cut a watermelon in half lengthwise. Scoop out the melon and fill with raspberry sherbet. Dot with chocolate chips in such a way that they look like watermelon seeds. It made a beautiful colored picture in the magazine, they tell me, and I know my guests rave when I serve it as both centerpiece and dessert. You see I freeze this, and take it out just before inviting guests to the table. It defrosts perfectly in time for dessert. Before I say good-bye to tamales, I must not forget to mention that the sweet ones or *Tamales Dulces* (page 147) are served at *meriendas* with Mexican chocolate. Why not have such an affair some late afternoon instead of another cocktail or tea party?

TOSTADA PARTY

Probably all of you have found that the great American snack favorite, the sandwich, is a satisfying answer to what to serve large groups. By the same token, I give *tostadas* parties—once for a mere 200! That number couldn't fit into my home, or yours, either, I don't suppose, but you can see that this party is well adapted for club suppers, too. To get down to cases, here's how to organize one: Fry tortillas the day before the party and get busy preparing the fillings, of which you will find many on page 178. Sometimes I have a friend type or write suggested combinations on cards. They are helpful if your guests have never met a *tostada* before, and they are a conversation piece, too. Just before party time, heap a large basket with *tostadas* (reheat them in oven if they aren't still crisp). Set out a nice selection of fillings in individual bowls. Be sure there's plenty of refried beans, a platter with cooked vegetables in French dressing, shredded lettuce, and for sure a choice of chile sauces. Your guests can have a fine time "building" their own *tostadas,* and you can be one of those truly carefree hostesses. Practically any beverage is good with them. If you want to go Mexican all the way, top it off with Mexican chocolate and assorted Mexican cookies.

MERIENDA

Mexican friends tease me considerably because of the liberties I've taken with the *merienda,* which is sort of the snack time of the early evening. I say that we don't have the same clocks in our stomachs here and go right ahead and call my buffet suppers *meriendas.* I start by inviting a few friends, but with so many wonderful ones, I never know when to stop and often end up serving 40 or 50. I've been told often enough I always have too much food, so I won't be hurt if you don't serve all the dishes I do at your *merienda.*

Just for your guidance, here goes with a typical *merienda* menu of 650 Victoria Street, San Francisco:

Appetizers:	*Ensalada de Coliflor* (page 195)
	Alcachofas en Salsa de Mostaza (page 197)
	Ensalada de Frijol (page 197)
	Tomatoes stuffed with *Guacamole* (page 8)
	Aceitunas Rellenas (page 20)
	Carnitas (page 10)
Main Dishes:	*Lengua a la Vinagreta* (page 102)
	Carne Margarita (page 100)
	Paella a la Valenciana (page 107)
	Arroz con Jocoqui (page 110)

Tacos de Gallina con Salsa de Chipotle (page 138)
Empanadas de Picadillo (pages 88, 173)

Accompaniments: *Quesadillas* (page 148)
Frijoles Refritos (page 114)
Chile sauces (pages 163–171)
Tostaditas (page 128)

Desserts: *Torta Borracha* (page 221)
Flan (page 207)
Mexican cookies (page 226)
Fruits (pages 231–232)

Beverages: Coffee
Red and white table wine
Beer
Mexican chocolate (page 234)

COMIDA PARA INVITADOS

(Dinner for Guests)

This is a formal, sit-down dinner. I'm going to try to give you a menu as typically Mexican as possible, and yet adaptable to our way of life. We are going to start with a *tequila* cocktail. You may select the one you like from the beverage category. Appetizers should accompany it. I suggest *Guacamole* (page 8) with *Tostaditas* (page 128) because it's a great favorite with everyone, and *Tomatitos Con Ostiones* (page 15).

Knowing that our meals are not complete without salads, I'm giving you a few suggestions, even though they are not often served with this meal in Mexico. I generally serve a variety of salads in a Lazy Susan. *Ensalada de Frijol* (page 197) plus pimientos with sour cream or cucumbers with cream cheese, which you'll find under salad suggestions on page 194. I like to serve

Quesadillas (page 148) made small, as an accompaniment to the salad.

Next would be a *Sopa Aguada* (liquid soup). A nice one would be *Sopa de Tomate y Aguacate* (page 28).

After soup, *Pescado a la Veracruzana* (page 55) or *Risoles de Camaron* (page 50).

For an entree, I suggest *Ternera Mechada* (page 98), accompanied by *Peritas de Papa* (page 183). Or, if you prefer chicken, *Pollos Deshuesados* (page 62) with *Bolas de Papa de Lujo* (page 182).

For a dessert, the famous *Flan* (page 207), or the equally popular *Natilla* (page 209).

Decorations for the table at affairs with a Mexican air? A sombrero filled with fruits or flowers, maybe. Red, white, and green candles or flowers to tie in with the national colors. An arrangement of cacti. An *olla* or other Mexican pottery with fruit or flowers. And for your fancy parties, red roses or carnations.

One more thing I promised myself to answer in this book. What wines with Mexican foods? I think that is pretty much up to individual tastes, but with the dishes which are highly flavored, a red table wine would be the better choice. With fish, cheese, and chicken dishes of mild flavor, a nicely chilled white table wine would be complimentary. For fiesta days, champagne is highly favored. If you want to know any more, just write to the Wine Institute, 717 Market Street, San Francisco, because that's where I got this information. After all, how can one who doesn't drink be a wine expert?

Barbacoa

❦ (Barbecue)

The old-time barbecue of Mexico was, and is, quite an event. Usually a *barbacoa de Domingo,* it is held on Sunday, or sometimes on other holidays, and is a far cry from the modern outdoor cookery that is usually called a barbecue in the United States. Although Mexicans, too, have taken to this new type of cooking, using built-in or portable charcoal grills, they still love their huge outdoor events at which the entire town or village often turns out. It is a picturesque affair, patterned after the method of cooking used by primitive man the world over, and still cherished in many places—the clambake of New England and the *luau* of the Hawaiian Islands being good examples. The food is cooked in a hole in the ground. The Mexican *barbacoa* has one touch of its very own: where the Hawaiians use *ti* leaves, and the Yankees seaweed, the Mexicans use the big fleshy leaves of the *maguey* plant. First a hole is dug—usually one about four feet deep. The sides of this are plastered with mud. In the hole go light porous stones, topped with a fire. When the wood has become ashes, the *maguey* leaves are roasted until tender and used to line the sides of the hole; their tops are laid back over the surface of the ground. A grate is then put over the ashes, and on top of it a pot with stock and garbanzos, rice, vegetables, and of course, chiles. Next comes the meat—lamb or kid, mutton or beef. The soft *maguey* leaves that are on the ground are folded over, a sheet of wood or metal is added, then another layer of mud. On top of this imposing heap a fire is built and kept burning for about five hours. Then comes the feast! The savory meat, along with some of the vegetable mixture, is served with a "drunken" sauce, so-called because strong *pulque* is used in it, as well as garlic, chiles, onions, olive oil, and salt. *Pulque* is also served as a beverage, at least to the adults, and soon the party is a merry one!

Today, Mexicans cook poultry and meats over outdoor charcoal grills, as we do. But because they do not have as tender beef as we have, they are apt to use ground meat, chicken, or turkey. However, their *salsa fria,* or cold sauce, has become a great favorite in the West to serve with broiled steaks and hamburgers. Other sauces, too, such as *chipotle* (page 168) and *tomatillo* (page 166) have become a part of American barbecue cooks' repertoires. Here are a few Mexican recipes that are particularly suitable for outdoor cooking. I do not attempt to tell you how to build a fire or spit a roast. The subject is a book in itself.

CARNE MOLIDA CON CHILE Y QUESO
(Hamburgers with Chile and Cheese)

Season 2 pounds of ground beef with 2 teaspoons of salt and a little black pepper. Add ¼ cup of red wine, ¼ cup of finely minced onion, and 1 egg. Form into 6 large fat balls. In the middle of each poke a good-sized cube of Jack cheese wrapped with half a peeled green chile. Flatten ever so slightly, put in a hinged broiler, and cook over hot coals for about 4 or 5 minutes on each side, or longer if you want it well done. Serve these with *frijoles refritos* (114) hot *tortillas* (126) and sliced tomatoes sprinkled with salt, pepper, and a powdering of orégano. *Bueno!* Serves 6.

CHULETAS

(Beef Cutlets)

2 *pounds ground beef*	1 *medium-sized onion,*
2 *teaspoons salt*	*chopped*
1 *clove garlic*	¼ *teaspoon cumin*
4 *slices bread*	¼ *teaspoon black pepper*

Mash garlic with salt; soak bread in water and squeeze dry; combine all ingredients and mix well. Form into flat oblong cakes and mark ridges with a fork. (This is to make them look as if they were ground on a *metate.*) Brush lightly with olive oil and put in a hinged broiler. Cook quickly on both sides, about 8 to 10 minutes in all. Serve with *salsa fria.* Serves 8.

ASADO DE GUAJOLOTE

(Roast Turkey)

Today, some Mexicans have taken to spit cookery, just as we have. This marinade may be used for lamb and beef as well as for turkey.

½ *cup dry sherry or white wine*	1 *clove garlic, mashed in*
¼ *cup oil*	1 *teaspoon salt*
1 *small onion, minced*	¼ *cup wine vinegar*
½ *teaspoon orégano*	

Combine all ingredients and use as a marinade or a baste. When roasting turkey it is used as a baste, and the juices are caught along with the excess, and used for a sauce. Brush a 16-pound turkey inside and out with the marinade. Truss and spit, making sure that the balance is right. Roast over a medium fire for 3 hours, or until the leg moves easily when pulled. During the roasting, baste occasionally. To make the sauce, skim off fat, mix 2 tablespoons of it with 2 tablespoons of flour, add 1½ cups of the juices and cook until slightly thickened.

ASADO AL PASTOR CON SALSA BORRACHA

(Shepherd's Roast with Drunken Sauce)

In Hidalgo, a specialty is this whole roasted mutton, called "Shepherd's Roast." Halves of mutton, specially trimmed, are hung over a wood fire on a crossbar, the ends of which are held by forked branches stuck into the ground. The meat is roasted slowly and turned so that it will cook evenly. Toward the end of the cooking, when the red juices stop running, the meat is basted with melted butter. It is served with *salsa borracha*. I roast a leg of mutton on a spit, over charcoal, and serve it with this adaptation of the salsa. In it I use *tequila* instead of *pulque,* as it is much easier to get in the United States.

Spit a large leg of mutton (or use lamb if you prefer) and roast it over a medium charcoal fire until done to your liking (1½ to 2½ hours). Serve with *salsa borracha* (below) and *frijoles* (page 113).

SALSA BORRACHA

4 dried chiles pasillas   2 pickled chiles serranos
1½ cups water   2 ounces dry cheese
2 cloves garlic   ½ cup tequila
½ cup olive oil   2 teaspoons salt
1 large onion, cut in chunks 1 tablespoon wine vinegar

Parch the dark red dried chiles pasillas in an ungreased heavy
skillet for a few minutes, turning so that they will not burn.
Remove stems and seeds, and cover with the water. In about an
hour, put in a blender with the remaining ingredients and ½ cup
of the water in which the chiles were soaked. Blend until smooth,
add remaining chile water, and serve. I have purposely made the
sauce mild. If you wish, you may add 3 or 4 more chiles serranos
for extra heat!

ARRECHERA ADOBADA

(Barbecued Skirt Steak)

I find skirt steak to be one of the best flavored. It may be im-
proved by letting it stand for several hours in a small amount
of vinegar, orégano, garlic, salt, and pepper. Often I just soak it
in lemon juice, then season and broil. It is not always easy to
find, so you may have to order it ahead from your butcher. Flank
steak could be used, instead.

1 skirt steak   1 teaspoon orégano, rubbed
  Salt and pepper   1 tablespoon vinegar
1 clove garlic, mashed or   2 tablespoons oil
  pressed

Combine salt, pepper, garlic, orégano, vinegar, and oil. Let steak marinate in this for an hour, then broil over hot coals, 3 or 4 minutes on each side. Brush with marinade before turning. Carve in thin diagonal slices.

POLLO ENCANELADO

(Cinnamon Chicken)

I suspect that this recipe has a background other than Mexican, but it is very popular below the border. Do try it—it is extra good!

½ cup sherry	1 small clove garlic, crushed or
2 teaspoons cinnamon	pressed
⅓ cup honey	Salt
2 tablespoons lemon juice	1 frying chicken, disjointed

Blend sherry, cinnamon, honey, lemon juice, garlic, and salt. Pour over chicken pieces, mixing so they are well coated. Let stand in the refrigerator for several hours, or overnight. Broil chicken over charcoal until tender, basting with any remaining marinade. This will take 40 minutes or longer, because it should not be cooked too close to the coals as the mixture tends to brown quite readily. If the marinade thickens during cooking, the pan drippings can be thinned with a little additional wine or broth to keep them from burning. Serves 4.

SALSA DE LEGUMBRES FRESCAS

(Fresh Garden Relish)

This relish is second cousin to the popular *salsa fria.* The brown sugar, in Mexico, is called *piloncillo,* which is a rather crudely refined sugar that has little drops like molasses throughout it. We can use dark brown sugar here. This is served with charcoal-broiled foods, as is *guacamole* (page 8).

2 large peeled tomatoes, diced	2 tablespoons brown sugar (packed)
1 peeled cucumber, diced	⅓ cup vinegar
½ cup diced green pepper or green chile	1 teaspoon salt
	½ teaspoon celery seed
⅓ cup finely-chopped onion	½ teaspoon black pepper

Combine all ingredients and mix lightly. Let stand several hours before serving. Makes about 3 cups.

SALSA DE VINO PARA CORDERO

(Wine Marinade for Lamb Chops)

Here is a very good marinade for lamb chops and chickens that are to be broiled over charcoal.

1 cup sauterne or other white table wine	½ teaspoon salt
	¼ teaspoon powdered thyme
2 tablespoons wine vinegar	¼ teaspoon powdered rosemary
1 tablespoon chopped, peeled green chiles	1 small clove garlic, crushed

Combine all ingredients. To use, pour over lamb chops and let stand a few hours, or overnight, in the refrigerator. Drain thoroughly and broil over hot coals, basting occasionally with the marinade. Lamb chops 1-inch thick will take from 8 to 25 minutes, depending upon how well done you like them. Split broilers will take about 30 minutes—perhaps a little longer if they are large or very cold when you start the broiling. This makes enough marinade for 8 chops or 2 split chickens.

ACCOMPANIMENTS FOR BARBECUE-COOKED MEATS

Both *frijoles refritos* and *tortillas* are naturals with barbecued meats and poultry, but so, too, are some of the *sopa secas. Sopa seca de tortilla,* for instance, and *sopa seca de arroz.* Garbanzos, also, are good with these outdoor meals. Any simple salad may be served at barbecues, but I think I prefer one of avocados, or avocado and tomato, or avocado and papaya. As for vegetables, the most appropriate are roasted corn or *colache,* and nothing could be better for dessert than some quince paste and Jack cheese, unless it was some guava shells stuffed with *queso fresco,* or cream cheese. Actually, any food tastes better when cooked and eaten outdoors, and no cuisine in the world fits better with outdoor parties than Mexican. Its gusty flavored and piquant sauces are just exactly right for lusty outdoor appetites.

Dias de Fiesta
Mexicanos

❦ (Mexican Holidays)

It's not really true, as some visitors to Siesta Land have observed, that every day is a holiday in Mexico. There are lots and lots of them, though, and since fun and food just naturally go together, practically every special day has its special dishes. Don't worry, I'm not attempting to cover all the holidays—I do believe a whole book could be written about them—but I do want to tell you a little about the principal ones and a bit more about their accompanying foods. Away we go!

Perhaps the most colorful fiesta of all is Independence Day or *Diez y Seis de Septiembre* (September 16th). Bands, fireworks, dancing, parades, and eating all add up to a large time for all. This is no day to stay home and cook, for you might miss something. Most people eat out that night if they don't any other time in the year. The shout of independence (*Grito de Independencia*) resounds from border to border at 11 in the evening, and before and after that the outdoor food stands are crowded with customers. The bill of fare features *Antojitos Mexicanos* (Mexican specialties to you)—*gorditas, tacos, tortas compuestas, tamales, quesadillas,* and such.

In direct contrast to the gaiety of the national holiday is the unique and somewhat ghoulish observance of *El Dia de Todos Santos,* or All Saints' Day, November 1st. To show you how closely allied are food and holidays, I'll just mention an old custom. On the eve of All Saints', a fancy table was set up for the loved ones who had died. The menu included all the favorite foods of the departed. I have my doubts that this is practiced even in the remote villages now, but there is still a significant sweet bread associated with this day. It is called *Pan de Muerto* or Bread of the Dead, and you'll find the recipe for it on page 222. Hot chocolate, coffee or *atole* are served with it in the morning and evening. In keeping with the spirit of the day, even toys and candies shaped like tombstones, skulls, and skeletons are sold in the stores.

The Mexicans like Christmas so much that they celebrate it for nine days or nights before December 25th. I must say I love the pageantry of this observance, called *Posadas,* which is Spanish for "inns," and re-enacts the search for shelter by Mary and Joseph. It's a real show with groups of friends and neighbors as actors. Each evening a crèche is carried by several in the group, preferably those of good voice, for they carol as they go from house to house to find lodging for the crèche. Refusals, often a bit rough, are all part of the act. So, too, is the acceptance pre-arranged. This is quite necessary, for the lady of the hospitable house must be prepared to serve the crowd such delicacies as *tamales, taquitos, café con leche,* hot chocolate and *atole.* And there must be a *piñata* for the children, although grownups enjoy this, too. If you don't know what a *piñata* is, let me tell you. It begins with an *olla* or earthenware pot which must be filled with fruits, candies, and unbreakable toys. This is concealed by a cardboard and decorated with paper to represent animals, boats, flowers, persons, or what would you. Some are simply fantastic and all of them are enchanting, I think. Anyway, during the *posadas,* the *piñata* is hung in the patio, often suspended from a tree. In many homes, prayers and singing precede the *piñata* party. Others carry out the delightful custom of providing small colored candles for every guest. This makes for a dramatic entrance to the patio, with each carrying a lighted candle. But now for the real fun. The children are blindfolded and given a cane or stick with which to try to break the *piñata*. I remember the song which we used to sing while the *piñata* party was in full swing and it went something like this:

> *Hit it, hit it*
> *Do not lose your aim*
> *Because if you do*
> *You'll lose your way.*

It sounds better in Spanish, I hope, but isn't it kind of cute? There's lots of "horse play" going on meanwhile, for the rope from which the *piñata* is suspended is pulled or shoved away by those without blindfolds to prevent its being broken too soon. When it breaks and showers its treasures, the children take to the ground (sometimes covered with carpet for the event) to gather the goodies.

The last *posada* is on December 24th and is marked by an elaborate midnight supper: Turkey Stuffed with Chestnuts (page 59), *Pescado Frio en Salsa de Piñón* (page 53), and Christmas Eve Salad (page 194) all being traditional.

You know how often you run across radishes in Mexican recipes. If you don't, you haven't read many of mine. In Oaxaca, Christmas Eve is also known as "Radish Night," and the radish is glorified like anything. They are cut in countless shapes—some are works of art—and used to decorate the small stands or restaurants around the square. Another custom that is quite untidy but unusual concerns *buñuelos* (page 220). On Radish Night or Christmas Eve, vendors serve them in cracked or imperfect Oaxaca dishes, which they save all year. It is traditional to eat the *buñuelo*, then break the dish. Can't you imagine what a heap of broken crockery needs to be swept up the next day?

Holiday dishes are starred at the New Year's Eve midnight supper and believe me there is a magnificent array: Turkey, duck, fish, *tamales,* salads, Mexican drinks, champagne and a whole gallery of desserts (lots of which you'll find in my book).

Christmas comes twice a year to some of the fortunate children of Mexico, for January 6th is celebrated as *El Dia de Los Santos Reyes,* the arrival of the kings to Bethlehem with gifts for the infant Jesus. Kiddies put their shoes outside the door or on the balconies, so the kings will leave them toys when passing by, and you'd be surprised how it works. Traditionally, *Rosca de Reyes* (page 212) is served on this holiday, and here I go again with a story. A small porcelain doll or sometimes a large bean is baked in the cake, and the person who finds it is crowned king or queen and may choose a partner for the evening. That sounds fine, but this same person must also have a party to which all of the people present are invited. The date is set for February 2nd and the party is called *Dia de la Candelaria.* When the doll is not found, everyone is accused of swallowing it so he (or could be she) won't have to give the party. *Mucho* fun, I'll tell you.

Another time Mexicans indulge in good-natured mischief is on Mardi Gras, the day before Ash Wednesday, as you are aware. Eggs figure in this, but not just ordinary ones. These are called *cascarones,* and you'd love them, for they are charmingly decorated egg shells. Although similar to the ones you see here at Easter, they are tricky and for a purpose. A quarter-sized piece of shell is carefully cut from the top, the inside is removed, and then the shell is filled with confetti and sometimes a drop of perfume, too. Tissue paper is pasted over the hole and lots of time is spent beautifying them up with dyes or paints. Now what happens? After all this work, the sweet little *cascarones* are broken over the heads of unsuspecting friends, showering them with confetti during Mardi Gras celebration! What a waste of pretty eggs, I think, but it makes for much laughter and that's good for everyone.

During Lent, lots of fish and egg and cheese dishes are served, of course. There is a liberal sprinkling of Lenten dishes in this book. I'd say the two most characteristic are *Tortas de Camaron* (page 57) and *Capirotada* (page 228).

If you are in Mexico the Saturday before Easter, you'll see a strange sight, around ten o'clock in the morning. The day is known as *Sábado de Gloria* and it commemorates Judas's betrayal of Jesus. Grotesque images of Judas, fashioned out of papier-mâché or made like scarecrows, are burned to the accompaniment of popping firecrackers. Although no special foods enter into the lively show, here again everyone is downtown and the sidewalk stands do a brisk business.

Easter Sunday is a day of feasting for sure. All the fiesta foods are in order, but *Mole de Guajolote* is on most tables. That brings me to a logical ending for this chapter. Of all the holiday dishes, turkey in *mole* sauce is the most important, I believe. It is served not only on Easter and other holidays, but on birthdays, anniversaries, weddings or at any very special party. Follow my recipe on page 61 and I feel reasonably sure you'll understand why the dish is so esteemed.

Most sincerely I believe that special days and special foods add many pleasures to family life. That's why I do hope you'll be inspired by this little chapter and borrow a few of these holiday customs from your neighbors to the South.

Index

T